Cr

DATE DUE

APR 0 1 2006			

F   S

T   LY

Creation, Evolution, & Modern Science: Probing the Headlines That Impact Your Family

© 2000 by Probe Ministries

Published by Kregel Publications, a division of Kregel, Inc., P.O. Box 2607, Grand Rapids, MI 49501. Kregel Publications provides trusted, biblical publications for Christian growth and service. Your comments and suggestions are valued.

For more information about Kregel Publications, visit our web site: www.kregel.com

ISBN 0-8254-2033-4

Printed in the United States of America

1 2 3 4 5 / 04 03 02 01 00

Contents

Foreword

Working with Probe Ministries, I have been impressed by the dedication and intellectual integrity its leaders display as they awaken sleeping minds to the truth of the gospel and to the extent to which our universities have repudiated truth.

There are plenty of Christian minds out there. Too often those minds have not been properly developed. In the late twentieth century, Christians did a fairly good job of addressing the hearts and emotions of students, no small accomplishment. What even the best evangelists often couldn't do, though, was to penetrate the intellectual culture of our universities with a solid intellectual platform that could stand up to the indoctrination in naturalist thinking. The gospel won a lot more hearts than it did minds. Unfortunately, the products of this naturalistic indoctrination now occupy the pews of our churches. Often these people are not even aware of the serious imbalance between their hearts and their minds.

Today, a new intellectual movement is making solid gains throughout Christian and secular educational institutions. The Intelligent Design movement starts with the recognition that "In the beginning was the Word," and "In the beginning God created." Establishing that point isn't enough, but it is absolutely essential to the rest of the gospel message. The contrary starting point, taken for granted in our universities and our culture, is, "In the beginning were the particles, and the impersonal laws of physics." That starting point never leads anyone to know God, or to appreciate the reality of sin and idolatry, or to know that we need a savior.

Get the starting point wrong, and everything is wrong; from the right starting point, the Truth has a chance to speak. The Truth really *will* speak for itself, because the Truth is a person, not merely an idea.

Christians have been absorbed for too long in Christian subculture arguments. We need to unite around the most fundamental truths and learn to proclaim those truths in a way that will get the attention of people whose minds have been put to sleep by naturalistic philosophies and pseudo-scientific theories. Once we establish the essential point that the Word really was "in the beginning," and that all the good scientific and philosophical arguments support that conclusion, we will have achieved a monumental breakthrough. After that, we will have plenty of time to discuss the remaining issues about how to interpret (and reconcile with science) the first few chapters of Genesis. We will approach those discussions in a better (and thus more Christian) frame of mind for having the experience of working together to defeat the idolatrous naturalistic dogmas that dominate our culture.

I pray that this book will inspire today's parents, teachers, students, and others who desire to know real truth, to go far beyond the starting point that we are in the process of establishing.

—PHILLIP E. JOHNSON
Jefferson E. Peyser Professor of Law
University of California, Berkeley

Contributors

Ray Bohlin is the executive director of Probe Ministries. He is a graduate of the University of Illinois (B.S., zoology), North Texas State University (M.S., population genetics), and the University of Texas at Dallas (M.S., Ph.D., molecular and cell biology). He is a coauthor of the book *Natural Limits to Biological Change* and has published numerous journal articles. He was named a 1997–98 Research Fellow of the Discovery Institute's Center for the Renewal of Science and Culture.

Sue Bohlin is an associate speaker with Probe. She attended the University of Illinois and Trinity Evangelical Divinity School and has been a Bible teacher and Christian speaker for more than twenty years. In addition to being a professional calligrapher, she also manages Probe's web site.

Rich Milne is a former research associate with Probe. He has a B.A. in English from the University of California, Berkeley, and a Th.M. from Dallas Theological Seminary. Currently, Rich coordinates information services and maintains the web site for East-West Ministries in Dallas, Texas. He continues to study science and the arts as a mirror of culture.

Rick Wade is a research associate with Probe. He has a B.A. in communications (radio broadcasting) from Moody Bible Institute and an M.A. (cum laude) in

Christian thought (theology/philosophy of religion) from Trinity Evangelical Divinity School, where his studies culminated in a thesis on the apologetics of Carl F. H. Henry.

Editor's Note

As you read through the chapters of this book, you may notice that the authors often, with little or no comment, use the traditional old-earth and old-universe system of dating matter. It would be easy to conclude that Probe Ministries unquestioningly accepts this theory. This is not the case. Probe takes no official stand on this critical controversy among Christians. The reason for our position is explained in chapter 15, entitled "Christian Views of Science and Earth History." I would like to add two further comments.

First, it is easier to show how insufficient the theory of evolutionary mechanisms is if we examine it from within the standard evolutionary time frame. In other words, by taking the position that the earth is millions or billions of years old, we can show that mere evolutionary processes could never produce the complex specificity of living organisms, nor could it generate life's amazing diversity.

Second, the authors of the various chapters in this book, myself included, are decidedly undecided about the age of the earth. We all have opinions and leanings, but we can see advantages and disadvantages on both sides. We have good friends, brothers and sisters in Christ, in both camps. It is most discomforting to watch fellow believers wrangle over this question. The critical problem before us is not the age of the earth and the universe. The critical problem is the stranglehold Darwinism has over the minds of the scientific community and beyond. It is paramount that Christians unite to meet this common foe. God the Father, through His Son Jesus Christ, is still the Creator, whether He took six days ten thousand years ago to create the earth or accomplished the same task over the course of 15 billion years.

Please be patient with our position—or our lack of one, if you prefer. We are acting according to our consciences. Working together in this way is a strategy that has borne fruit and, we trust, will continue to do so in the days to come.

—Ray Bohlin
General Editor

Part 1

The Different Faces of Evolution

1

The Five Crises in Evolutionary Theory

Ray Bohlin

The growing credibility crisis in Darwinian theory is becoming more apparent all the time. The work of creationists and other non-Darwinians is growing and finding an increasingly receptive ear. In this discussion I want to elaborate on what I believe are the five critical areas where Darwinism and evolutionary theory in general are failing. They are (1) the insubstantial basis for the Darwinian mechanism of evolution, (2) the total failure of origin-of-life studies to produce a workable model, (3) the inability of evolutionary mechanisms to explain the origin of complex adaptations, (4) the bankruptcy of the blind-watchmaker hypothesis, and (5) the biological evidence that the rule in nature is morphological stability over time, not constant change.

Much of the reason for the theory of evolution's privileged status has been the confusion over what people mean when they use the word *evolution.* It is a slippery term. If *evolution* simply means "change over time," there is no controversy. Peppered moths, Hawaiian drosophila fruit flies, and even Galapagos finches are clear examples of change over time. If you say that this form of evolution is a fact—well, so be it. But many scientists extrapolate beyond this. Because "change over time" is a fact, the argument goes, then it must also be a fact that moths, fruit flies, and finches all evolved from a remote common ancestor.

The real question, therefore, is: Where do moths, flies, and finches come from in the first place? Common examples of natural selection, acting on present genetic variation, do not tell us how we have come to have horses, wasps, woodpeckers, and the enormous variety of living animals. Evolutionists will tell you that this is where mutations enter the picture. But mutations do not improve the scenario either. In speaking of all the mutation work done with bacteria over several decades, the great French zoologist and evolutionist Pierre Paul Grassé, said: "What is the use of their unceasing mutations if they do not change? In sum, the mutations of bacteria and viruses are merely hereditary fluctuations around a median position; a swing to the right, a swing to the left, but no final evolutionary effect."[1]

When I speak of evolution or Darwinism, it is the origin of new biological forms, new adaptive structures, morphological and biochemical novelties that I am referring to. This is precisely what has not been explained by science. When faced with the task of explaining the origin of complex adaptations such as the vertebrate limb, sexual reproduction, the tongue of the woodpecker, or the reptilian hard-shelled egg, scientists usually give a litany of reasons why these structures are beneficial to the organisms. More precisely, the selective advantage of these structures is offered as the reason why they evolved. Yet, it is not sufficient for evolutionists to explain the function of a particular structure. What is necessary is to explain the mechanistic origin of these structures!

Surprisingly, even in well-studied examples of evolutionary change such as Darwin's finches on the Galapagos Islands, we do not know what genetic changes have taken place. The morphological shifts have been well established but no attempt has yet been made to understand the genetic component of these changes.

While I will elaborate on this difficulty later in the discussion, it is important to note that natural selection never explains how organisms adapt to minor changes in their environment. Natural selection allows organisms to do what God commanded them to do—to be fruitful and multiply. Natural selection does not, however, explain how complex adaptations arose in the first place.

The Origin of Life

We have been led to believe that it is not too difficult to conceive of a mechanism whereby organic molecules can be manufactured in a primitive earth and organized into living, replicating cells. In fact, the ease with which this can (allegedly) happen is the foundation for the popular belief that there are numerous planets in our galaxy and universe that contain life. Nothing could be further from the truth.

Early experiments suggested that it might be relatively simple to produce some of the building blocks of life—such as amino acids, the components of proteins. However, the euphoria of the Miller-Urey experiment of 1953 has given way to a paradigm crisis in origin-of-life research. The wishful yet workable atmosphere of ammonia, hydrogen, methane, and water vapor has been replaced by the more realistic but stingy atmosphere of nitrogen, carbon dioxide, carbon monoxide, hydrogen sulfide, and hydrogen cyanide—the stuff that volcanoes belch out. This atmosphere poses a difficult challenge. Molecules relevant for life would be much more rare. Even more damaging is the possible presence of molecular oxygen in the atmosphere from the breakup of water vapor. Molecular oxygen would poison any reaction leading to biologically significant molecules. The very existence of a prebiotic or primordial soup has been negated by the evidence: "Furthermore, no geological evidence indicates an organic soup, even a small organic pond, ever existed on this planet. It is becoming clear that however life began on earth, the usually conceived notion that life emerged from an oceanic soup of organic chemicals is a most implausible hypothesis. We may with fairness call this scenario 'the myth of the prebiotic soup.'"[2]

Coacervates, the "RNA world," and other scenarios all have serious flaws obvious to everyone in the field except those who continue to work within these particular theories. Some have privately called this predicament a paradigm crisis. There is no central model, just numerous ego-driven theories. Experiments in which researchers try to simulate the early earth have been severely criticized. These experiments generally hedge their bets by using purified reactants, isolated energy sources, and exaggerated energy levels—procedures which unrealistically drive the reaction toward the desired product and protect the products from the destructive effects of the energy sources that produced them in the first place.[3]

Klaus Dose summed up the real situation rather well: "More than 30 years of experimentation on the origin of life in the fields of chemical and molecular evolution have led to a better perception of the immensity of the problem of the origin of life on earth rather than to its solution. At present all discussions on principal theories and experiments in the field either end in stalemate or in a confession of ignorance."[4]

But all of these difficulties together, staggering as they are, are not the real problem. The major difficulty in the field of chemical evolution is how to account for the informational code of DNA without intelligence being a part of the equation. DNA carries the genetic code—the genetic blueprint for constructing and maintaining a biological organism. We often use the terms of "language" to describe DNA's activity: DNA is "transcribed" into RNA; RNA is "translated" into protein; geneticists speak of the genetic "code." All these words imply intelligence. The DNA informational code requires intelligent preprogramming, yet a purely naturalistic beginning does not provide such input. Chemical experiments may be able to construct small sequences of nucleotides that form small molecules of DNA, but this doesn't make them mean anything. There is no source for the informational code in a strictly naturalistic origin of life. "But scientific investigations of the origin of life have clearly led us to conclude that an intelligent cause may, in the final analysis, be the only rational possibility to explain the enigma of the origin of life: information."[5]

The Inability to Account for Complex Adaptations

Next, I must deal with the failure of evolutionary theories to explain the biological world we see before us. Perhaps the single greatest obstacle for evolutionary biologists is the unsolved problem of morphological and biochemical novelty. In other words, some aspects of evolutionary theory describe accurately how existing organisms are well adapted to their environments, but they do a very poor job of explaining just how the necessary adaptive structures came about in the first place.

Darwinian explanations of complex structures, such as the eye and the incredible tongue of the woodpecker, fall far short of realistically explaining how these structures arose by mutation and natural selection. The origin of the eye, in particular, caused Darwin no small problem. His only suggestion was to look at the variety of eyes in nature, some more complex and versatile than others, and imagine a gradual sequence leading from simple eyes to more complex eyes. However, even the great Harvard evolutionist, Ernst Mayr, admits that the various eyes in nature are not really related to each other in some simple-to-complex sequence. Rather, he suggests that eyes probably had to evolve over forty different times in nature. Darwin's nightmare has never been solved. It has only been made forty times more frightening for the evolutionist.

British evolutionist Richard Dawkins recounts the work of Dan Nilsson and Susanne Pelger who demonstrated, by a computer model, the evolution of the camera eye. Surprisingly, they begin with three rather specialized layers of cells and proceed to show how the back of the eye can curve by gradual mutation. Where do the three layers of cells come from? The lens magically appears by "condensing" out of the clear vitreous mass. Yet Dawkins claims, "There is no sleight of hand here."[6]

In his 1987 book, *Theories of Life,* Wallace Arthur said, "One can argue that there is no direct evidence for a Darwinian origin of a body plan—black *Biston betularia* certainly do not constitute one! Thus in the end we have to admit that we do not really know how body plans originate."[7]

In a later book, Arthur emphasizes the conundrum of combining the Darwinian theory of the gradual accumulation of changes and developmental biology. The major differences between organisms, such as the those between mammals and insects (which are from different phyla), occur early in development. But the changes between these two organisms cannot have come about by accumulating mutations over millions of years. Darwinian changes generally occur late in embryonic development. Mutations dividing arthropods from chordates had to have happened very early in development when mutations are most harmful.

> This approach has important consequences for the neo-Darwinian view that major morphological differences between organisms from different higher taxa have been produced through gradual accumulation of very small changes. Specifically, while in a non-developmental approach it seems plausible that many small changes can indeed accumulate to give a larger one, in a developmentally explicit approach it is clear that *many late changes cannot accumulate to give an early one.*[8]

In 1992, Keith Stewart Thomson wrote in the *American Zoologist* that "while the origins of major morphological novelties remain unsolved, one can also view the stubborn persistence of macroevolutionary questioning . . . as a challenge to orthodoxy: resistance to the view that the synthetic theory tells us everything we need to know about evolutionary processes."[9]

Inability to explain major morphological novelties is not the only failing of evolutionary theory. Some argue that molecular structures are even more difficult to explain. The molecular architecture of the cell has recently been described by molecular biologist Michael Behe[10] as being composed of systems of irreducible complexity, systems that must have all the components present in order to be functional. The molecular workings of cilia, electron transport, protein synthesis, and cellular targeting readily come to mind. If the systems are irreducibly complex, how do they slowly build over long periods of time out of systems that are originally doing something else?

Over the last ten years, the *Journal of Molecular Evolution* has published hundreds of articles pertaining to molecular homology and phylogeny of various proteins and nucleic acids, yet it did not publish one article attempting to explain the origin of a single biomolecular system. Those who make molecular evolution their life's work are too busy studying the cytochrome *c* molecule in man in relation to the cytochrome *c* molecule in bacteria, rather than the more fundamental question of where cytochrome *c* came from in the first place!

Clearly, whether we are talking about major morphological novelties such as the wings of bats and birds, the swimming adaptations of fish and whales, the human eye, or the molecular submicroscopic workings of mitochondria, ribosomes, or cilia, evolutionary theory has failed to explain how such structures could arise by natural processes alone.

The Bankruptcy of the Blind-Watchmaker Hypothesis

In his 1986 book, *The Blind Watchmaker,* Richard Dawkins states, "Biology is the study of complicated things that give the appearance of having been designed for a purpose."[11] He explains that "natural selection is the blind watchmaker, blind because it does not see ahead, does not plan consequences, has no purposes in view. Yet the living results of natural selection overwhelmingly impress us with the appearance of design as if by a master watchmaker, impress us with the illusion of design and planning."[12]

Darwinism critic Philip Johnson has quipped that the watchmaker is not only blind but unconscious!

Dawkins later suggests just how this process may have brought about the development of wings in mammals. He says:

> How did wings get their start? Many animals leap from bough to bough, and sometimes fall to the ground. Especially in a small animal, the whole body surface catches the air and assists the leap, or breaks the fall, by acting as a crude aerofoil. Any tendency to increase the ratio of surface area to weight would help, for example flaps of skin growing out in the angles of joints . . . (It) doesn't matter how small and unwinglike the first wingflaps were. There must be some height, call it h, such that an animal would just break its neck if it fell from that height. In this critical zone, any improvement in the body surface's ability to catch the air and break the fall, however slight the improvement, can make the difference between life and death. Natural selection will then favor slight, prototype wingflaps. When these flaps have become the norm, the critical height h will become slightly

greater. Now a slight further increase in the
wingflaps will make the difference between
life and death. And so on, until we have
proper wings.[13]

This can sound seductively convincing at first. However, there are three faulty assumptions.[14]

The first doubtful assumption is that nature can provide
a chain of favorable mutations of the precise kind needed
to change forelimbs into wings in a continuous line of
development. What is the larger miracle, an instantaneous
change or a whole series of thousands of tiny changes in
the proper sequence?

The next assumption is "all things being equal." These
mutations must not have secondary harmful effects. How
is the creature's grasping ability compromised while these
wingflaps grow? These little shrewlike animals may slowly
be caught between losing their proficiency in the trees
before they can fully utilize their "developing" wings. Or
there might be some seemingly unrelated and unforeseen
effect that compromises their ability to survive.

A third faulty assumption is the analogy to artificial
selection. "If artificial selection can do so much in only a
few years," the refrain goes, "just think what natural selection can do in millions of years." But artificial selection
works because it incorporates foresight and conscious purpose, the absence of which is the defining qualities of the
blind watchmaker. In addition, artificial selection actually
demonstrates the limits to change since an endpoint in
the selection process is usually reached very quickly.

The blind watchmaker hypothesis, when analyzed carefully, falls into the category of fanciful stories. It is enter-
taining, but it bears no resemblance to reality.

The Prevalence of Stasis over Mutability

Biology has taught us that nature resists change much more effectively than it produces change. This is perhaps the most embarrassing biological phenomenon of all for evolutionists. The evidence of biology clearly points to stasis not evolution.

Rather than revealing organisms gradually evolving into other forms, the fossil record speaks of "sudden appearance" and "stasis." New types appear suddenly and then change very little after their appearance. Stephen Jay Gould of Harvard revealed that the rarity of gradual-change examples in the fossil record was the trade secret of paleontology.[15] Gould also refers to stasis as "data" in the paleontological sense.[16] These are significant observations. Darwin predicted that there would be innumerable transitional forms between species. But the reality of paleontology (the study of fossils) is that new forms appear suddenly with no hint of the "gradual" change predicted by evolution. Not only that, but once these new forms have appeared, they remain relatively unchanged up to the present day or until they become extinct.

Some animals and plants have remained the same for literally hundreds of millions of years. These "living fossils" can be more embarrassing for evolutionists than they care to admit. One creature in particular, the coelacanth, is very instructive. The first live coelacanth was found off the coast of Madagascar in 1938. Coelacanths were thought to have been extinct for 100 million years. Most evolutionists saw this discovery as a great opportunity to glimpse the workings of a tetrapod ancestor. Coelacanths resemble the proposed ancestors of amphibians. It was hoped that some clues could be derived from the modern coelacanth on how fish became preadapted for life on land. Not only was there a complete skeleton to examine, but a full set of internal organs to boot. The results of the study were very disappointing. The modern coelacanth showed no evidence of internal organs preadapted for use in a terrestrial environment. The coelacanth is a fish—nothing more, nothing less. Its bony fins are exceptionally well-designed paddles used for changing direction in a deep-sea environment, not the protolimbs of future amphibians.[17]

Nowhere is the problem of sudden appearance better demonstrated than in the Burgess Shale found in the Canadian Rockies. The Burgess Shale illustrates that in the Cambrian period (which evolutionists estimate as being over 540 million years ago) nearly all of the basic body plans (phyla) of animals existing on earth came into existence in a geological instant (defined as only 5 to 10 million years). No new phyla have appeared since that time (the Bryazoa are one possible exception, but many paleontologists believe they will eventually be found to originate in the Cambrian period). The Cambrian explosion, as it is called, is nothing less than astounding. Sponges, jellyfish, worms, arthropods (insects and crustaceans), mollusks (clams and snails), echinoderms (starfish and sand dollars), and many other stranger-than-fiction creatures all suddenly appeared in the Cambrian period without a hint of what they descended from nor even how they could all be related to each other. This is the opposite expectation of Darwinism, which would have predicted each new body plan emerging from preexisting phyla over long periods of time. The Cambrian explosion is a direct contradiction of Darwinian evolution.

If Darwin were alive today, I believe he would be terribly disappointed. There is less evidence for his theory now than in his own day. The possibility of the human eye evolving may have caused him to shudder, but the organization of the simplest cell is infinitely more complex. Perhaps a nervous breakdown would be more appropriate!

2

Human Fossils

Just So *Stories of Apes and Humans*

Ray Bohlin

I am reminded of a story of an inquisitive young girl who asked her parents where people come from. Her parents dutifully answered that God made man from the dust of the ground. A little later she asked what happened to people when they died. Her parents responded that their souls are destined for either heaven or hell but that their bodies will return to the dust of the ground from which they came. Well, several weeks later, the young scientist came running down the stairs with some exciting news! She had found a human under her bed, but she couldn't tell whether it was coming or going!

Australopithecines

The March 14, 1994, issue of *Time* magazine displayed a picture of *Homo erectus* on the cover with the title, "How Man Began: Fossil Bones from the Dawn of Humanity are Rewriting the Story of Evolution." The question of human origins fascinates us! Many people are intrigued by the idea that we descended from an apelike ancestor 7 million years ago. The field of paleoanthropology, the study of human fossils, embraces colorful personalities who compete for our allegiance to their particular evolutionary scheme. Mary and Louis Leakey, their son Richard Leakey, and Donald Johanson are all recognizable names in this enthralling field of study.

Reading *Time, Newsweek,* and *National Geographic* convinces many people that humans evolved from apelike ancestors. However, a now well-known 1991 Gallup poll indicates that 47 percent of adults in the United States, almost half, believe humans were created only ten thousand years ago and that only 9 percent, less than one in ten, believe humans are the result of an evolutionary process in which God played no part.[1] So who's fooling whom? I want to take a brief look at the evidence for human evolution. This is an engrossing topic with some surprising answers.

The story supposedly begins about 3.5 million years ago with the appearance of a group of animals collectively known as australopithecines. *Australo* meaning "southern" and *pithecines* meaning "apes." These "southern apes," initially discovered in South Africa, were small, apparently upright walking apes. Then around 2 million years ago, a new creature appeared that is now put into the genus *Homo—Homo habilis.* These creatures possessed the same stature of the australopithecines but had a slightly larger brain. It is also suggested that they used a few primitive tools. Next appeared the real star of human evolution, *Homo erectus. Homo erectus* possessed the skeletal frame of modern humans, though a little more robust, and its brain capacity was closer to humans than that of *Homo habilis. Homo erectus* used more advanced tools. These "almost" humans hung around, we're told, for over 1.5 million years when nearly modern humans (*Homo sapiens,* around four hundred thousand years ago) began to appear. Soon the offshoot

Neanderthals arose, and about the same time thoroughly modern humans appeared in the last one hundred thousand years.

While this is the standard story, it is far from convincing when all the data is considered. Take the australopithecines, for example. While there is still some debate whether these creatures walked upright at all, most anthropologists accept that they walked on two legs. But this is misleading if you don't know the rest of the story. The fact is that Lucy, the most famous australopithecine *(Australopithecus afarensis)*, was also mildly adapted to life in the trees. The evolutionist William Howells has said there is general agreement that Lucy's gait is *not* properly understood, and that it was *not* something simply transitional to ours.[2] If Lucy walked upright, it was a movement that was distinct from both apes and humans. Not exactly what you would expect from a transitional form. Lucy is simply an extinct ape with no clear connection to humans.

In addition, Roger Lewin clarifies the position of *A. afarensis,*

> Clearly, an adaptive shift occurred with *A. afarensis,* one that looks dramatic by comparison with modern apes. The proper comparison, however, must involve some of the Miocene apes from which the hominine clade might have derived. From this viewpoint, *A. afarensis* really does exhibit an apelike appearance, in terms of both anatomy and diet. It would have been different from a behavioral standpoint, because *A. afarensis* habitually walked on two legs.[3]

The Uncertainties of *Homo Erectus*

We have all seen the series of extinct creatures that leads from ape to man. Evolutionists confidently declare that while there may be a lot of details missing from the story, the basic outline is fairly complete. This all seems impressive. Yet, in his book, *Bones of Contention,* creationist Marvin Lubenow offers an important observation. "What is not generally known is that this sequence, impressive as it seems, is a very artificial and arbitrary arrangement because 1) some fossils are selectively excluded if they do not fit well into the evolutionary scheme; 2) some human fossils are arbitrarily downgraded to make them appear to be evolutionary ancestors when they are in fact true humans; and 3) some nonhuman fossils are upgraded to make them appear to be human ancestors."[4]

The australopithecines are a good example of Lubenow's third point. These extinct apes are trumpeted as human ancestors because of their crude bipedal walking ability. But nearly everything else about them is apelike. Explaining the origin of their bipedality would be no small evolutionary task. Even Richard Leakey admits as much in his book with Roger Lewin, *Origins Reconsidered.*[5] He says that the change from walking on four legs to walking on two legs would have required an extensive remodeling of the ape's bone and muscle architecture and of the overall proportion in the lower half of the body. Mechanisms of gait are different, mechanics of balance are different, functions of major muscles are different. An entire functional complex had to be transformed for efficient bipedalism to be possible.

Yet these immense changes are not documented from the fossil record.

A good example of Lubenow's second point, the arbitrary downgrading of human fossils to make them appear to be our ancestors, is *Homo erectus*. *Homo erectus* is said to have lived from around 1.7 million years ago to nearly four hundred thousand years ago. From its first appearance, *erectus* is acknowledged to have a fully human postcranial skeleton (that means everything but the head). But the brain size is given an evolutionary twist by saying that it only approaches the average for modern humans. In reality, *Homo erectus's* brain size is within the range of modern humans.

Throughout the course of their book, *Origins Reconsidered*,[6] Leakey and Lewin document an impressive array of characteristics that distinguish the apelike qualities of australopithecines from the human qualities of *Homo erectus*. Australopithecines are small in stature, only three to four feet tall, and the males are twice the size of the females. In *Homo erectus* and humans, the males are only 15 to 20 percent larger than females, and it is estimated that a juvenile *erectus* fossil, had he lived into adulthood, would have grown to a height of six feet.

In *Homo erectus*, all of the following characteristics display the human pattern, while in australopithecines, the ape pattern is evident: growth pattern, dental structure and development, facial structure and development, brain morphology, height-to-weight ratio, probable position of larynx based on the contours of the base of the skull making speech possible, and the size of the birth canal relative to the size of the adult brain.

Many of the differences between *Homo erectus* fossils and humans can be explained by the effects of inbreeding, dietary restrictions, and a harsh environment. But evolutionists need an intermediate, and *Homo erectus* is the only option available.

Neanderthals and the Paleontologists

In the field of paleoanthropology, the study of human fossils, we must approach the data and interpretations of the scientists involved with a careful and skeptical eye. There are a number of obvious reasons for this healthy skepticism. The most important reason is that they are looking for our evolutionary ancestors. If that is what they are looking for, then that is likely what they will report to have found. Such is human nature.

A second reason is that there is a great deal of competition among anthropologists. They are involved in a race to discover *the* missing link, which would mean immense fame and financial gain. The temptation to exaggerate the importance of their findings at the expense of others is very great.

Another reason for skepticism is that anthropologists are only able to compare plaster casts of fossils and measurements from printed material. The actual fossils are understandably considered too fragile and valuable to be handled directly all the time. However, plaster casts are sadly unable to reflect accurately many of the details needed for proper study. In 1984, the largest-ever collection of actual fossils was gathered from around the world at the American Museum of Natural History for the opening of the "Ancestors" exhibit. It was a unique opportunity for side-by-side comparisons and it took much persuasion to pull it off. The mounts for each skull or fragment were individually prepared, using plaster casts of the original fossils. Unfortunately, when the real fossils showed up, most of them did not fit! It is a myth that those who teach and write on human origins have actually held in their hands even a fraction of the original material.[7]

Evolutionists have been embarrassed on more than one

occasion by their evolutionary bias, their competition, and their lack of familiarity with the original fossils. A good example is the misinterpretation of Neanderthals. Though there is now much dispute over whether Neanderthals are a human subspecies or a completely different species, in the early part of the twentieth century there was unanimity in the belief that Neanderthals were brutish, stooped creatures who were more closely related to apes than to humans. That impression stood for over forty years. One of the first complete Neanderthal skeletons was found in a cave in France in 1908. It was given to the French paleontologist, Marcellin Boule to reconstruct. From the study of other fragmentary fossils, Boule had already formed an evolutionary bias that Neanderthals were not related to humans. Boule saw only the "primitive" traits of Neanderthals and ignored clear evidence of arthritis and rickets in the skeleton. Boule reconstructed the skeleton without the curves in the spine that allow humans to walk upright. He also placed the skull far forward so that it would have been difficult to look up as we do. Other miscues produced an individual who was little more than a shuffling hunchback. Because of Boule's reputation this reconstruction stood until 1957, when two scientists reexamined it and found his prejudicial mistakes. Their study concluded that Neanderthals, when healthy, stood erect and walked normally. Neanderthals were simply stronger, stockier members of the human family.[8]

Allowing the Facts to Speak

It is interesting to note certain pieces of fossil evidence that have either been ignored or stretched in order to not upset the accepted picture of human evolution. Creationist Marvin Lubenow, in his recent book, *Bones of Contention,* gives numerous examples of this kind of manipulation, and I'd like to discuss three of the most glaring incidents.

The first concerns a bone fragment of the lower end of the upper arm, near the elbow, that was found near Kanapoi, Kenya, in 1965 and has been given the designation, KP 271. What is unusual about this discovery is its estimated age of around 4.5 million years, unusual because it appears to be human, and humans are not supposed to have been around 4.5 million years ago. Consequently, this small piece of humerus is usually designated as *Australopithecus* because that is the only hominid species known to be in existence at that time. Lubenow quotes Harvard anthropologist William Howells in a stunning admission: "The humeral fragment from Kanapoi, with a date of about 4.4 million, could not be distinguished from Homo sapiens morphologically or by multivariate analysis by Patterson and myself in 1967. . . . We suggested that it might represent Australopithecus because at that time allocation to Homo seemed preposterous, although it would be the correct one without the time element."[9]

Donald Johanson and Blake Edgar, after casually commenting that recent finds at Kanapoi of a new species, *Australopithecus anamensis,* are dated at 3.9 to 4.2 million years, conclude that "a distal humerus found at Kanapoi in 1965 has now been attributed to this new species."[10] They curiously omit any discussion of the controversial nature of this fossil.

The only reason KP 271 is not listed as human is because it can't be, according to evolution.

Second, many have heard of a series of footprints found by Mary Leakey near Laetoli, Tanzania. Richard Leakey and Roger Lewin just gloss over them, calling them hominid footprints.[11] Lubenow documents that these footprints are identical to those made today by humans who always walk barefoot, yet these footprints are routinely classified as australopithecine. William Howells refers to the conclusions of Russell Tuttle from the University of Chicago and a leading expert on hominoid gates and limbs as saying that the footprints are nearly identical to those of modern humans and that australopithecine feet are significantly different. Tuttle suggests an undiscovered species made these prints. He can't say that a human made them because humans aren't supposed to have existed yet. In the words of evolutionist William Howells, "Here is something of an enigma."[12] Indeed! "Johanson and Edgar, while mentioning the controversy, simply reference a 1983 re-examination by Suwa and White claiming that adjusting for size allows the *A. afarensis* bones to fit the footprint."[13]

Finally, Lubenow documents the incredible saga of determining the date for Skull 1470.[14] Skull 1470 is very modern in its appearance but was found in rock previously dated at 2.9 million years, much too old for such a modern skull. So some scientists set out to determine a much later date. Lubenow recounts the back and forth wrangling over the issue. Several radioactive methods and paleomagnetism pointed to 2.9 million years, but other methods, including fission-track dating suggested a date of 1.9 million years. Ultimately the radioactive dates were tossed aside in favor of a date of 1.9 million years, a date that fit human evolution better, based on the certainty of the dates of pig evolution. Yes, pig evolution. To quote Lubenow, "The pigs won. . . . The pigs took it all. But in reality, it wasn't the pigs that won. It was evolution that won. In the dating game, evolution always wins."[15] This is in spite of the fact that elephant fossils in the formation suggest agreement with the older date!

A Creationist Perspective on Ancient Humans

Thus far we have been discussing some of the significant problems with evolutionary explanations of ancient human remains. But questions still remain. Many of these individuals do look very different from modern humans. Who are they? Where did they come from? Does any of this make sense from a creationist perspective? While we need to be careful not to overinterpret the data as we have accused evolutionists of doing, there are a few suggestions that make some sense.

The most obvious first step is to recognize that *Homo erectus,* archaic *Homo sapiens,* Neanderthals, and *Homo sapiens* form a continuum of the human family. The different forms represent genetic variations within a species and not distinct species. Many evolutionists themselves have difficulty drawing the line between these four different labels.

A group of human fossils from Kow Swamp, Australia, are no more than thirteen thousand years old yet their skulls contain many of the skull characteristics of *Homo erectus.* Some of the reasons for this involve cultural circumstances and not genetic differences. In other words, many of the characteristics of *Homo erectus* can be achieved in modern humans by lifestyle changes. These could include deliberate forehead compression, deformation due to inbreeding, modifications due to dietary deficiencies, and peculiarities.[16] The late Arthur Custance documents differences in the modern skulls of Eskimos due to the massive jaw muscles that are developed because of their diet.[17] Many of these differences would be labeled as primitive if dug up in some ancient riverbed, yet they exist in fully modern humans today.

Marvin Lubenow offers the interesting suggestion that many of these ancient humans are the remains of individuals within the first millennia after the flood of Noah.[18] Effects of the ice age, constant cloud cover (preventing Vitamin D formation and leading to rickets), a largely vegetarian and uncooked diet, and expression of local genetic variation could readily account for the many different, yet anatomically related, human forms. Are these ancient humans former apelike creatures that are evolving toward humans, or are they humans caught in a unique and harsh world that brought about numerous intraspecies variants? Evolutionists never bother to ask the latter question. A creationist perspective, in this case, may lead to ideas that evolutionists should look at. That is the value, in science, of a different perspective.

3

The Natural Limits to Biological Change

Ray Bohlin

One of the most significant questions in the origins debate concerns the nature of biological change. Can organisms change into an infinite array of creatures? Or are there genetically imposed limits to the amount of change that can take place? There are two major theories of evolutionary change: neo-Darwinism and punctuated equilibrium. As creationists, Lane Lester and I proposed in 1984 that, indeed, there are limits to change.[1] Theoretically, it may seem difficult to propose that immense variety can occur within a group of organisms while at the same time this variety is constrained within certain genetically induced limits. It may even seem contradictory. But in the intervening years, my belief in the proposal has only strengthened, and my confidence in any evolutionary mechanism to accomplish significant adaptational change has waned considerably.

The arguments against neo-Darwinism center around four topics: mutation, natural selection, population genetics, and paleontology. Our major objection to the role of mutations in evolutionary change is the clear lack of data to indicate that mutations really accomplish anything new. While some weird-looking fruit flies have been created in the laboratory, they are still fruit flies. Bacteria are still bacteria. The quotation from Pierre Paul Grassé, the great French evolutionist, is worth repeating. When commenting on the mutations of bacteria he said: "What is the use of their unceasing mutations if they do not change? In sum, the mutations of bacteria and viruses are merely hereditary fluctuations around a median position; a swing to the right, a swing to the left, but no final evolutionary effect."[2]

An evolutionary mechanism for the creation of new genetic material is also speculative and inadequate. The story goes that sometimes an extra copy of a gene arises due to a DNA duplication error. Evolutionists suggest that this extra gene can accumulate mutations and eventually code for a new gene with a different function. In reality, however, this fails to explain how an old gene that is out of the regulation loop (no active means to turn the gene on or off) takes on a new function. Also left out of the explanation is a mechanism for getting this new gene to be expressed again. And all of this is supposed to happen by the introduction of genetic mistakes into the gene and the regulatory apparatus.

Natural selection is a conservative process, not a creative one. The famous example of peppered moths teaches us how a species survives in a changing environment by possessing two varieties adapted to different conditions. (And even this now well-known story is losing its luster as an example of natural selection in action.[3]) Antibiotic resistance in bacteria only instructed us in the ingenious mechanisms of different bacteria to share the already existing genes for antibiotic resistance among themselves.

Decades of research in the science of population genetics have not helped the neo-Darwinist position. The data from protein and gene variation shed only a dim light on the major problem of evolution—the appearance of novel adaptations. The major contribution of population genetics has been to explain how an organism responds to minor environmental fluctuations. And even this can be clouded by fundamental differences in theory.

The data of paleontology have been elaborated at length elsewhere. Gradual, neo-Darwinian evolution is not observable across the board in the fossil record. The rarity of transitional forms has been called the trade secret of paleontology. While evolutionists will proudly point to examples of transitions in the fossil record, the reality is that these are always marked with great fanfare precisely because they are so rare. If Darwinian evolution is true, such transitions should be the rule, not the exception. Mutations, natural selection, genetics, and paleontology have all proved to be dead ends for Darwinism.

Obstacles to the Theory of Punctuated Equilibrium

As mentioned in chapter 1, the coelacanth is a fish that has existed for hundreds of millions of years, according to evolutionists, and was thought to resemble the ancestors of modern amphibians. However, research into its anatomy, physiology, and life history since its rediscovery off Madagascar in 1938 have revealed no clues to its possible pre-adaptation to a terrestrial existence.[4] The coelacanth has been used as an example of stasis—the long-term stability of new species—the first cornerstone in the theory of punctuated equilibrium. A second is the sudden appearance of new species. One doesn't have to look very far for statements by paleontologists pointing to the fact that transitional forms are traditionally absent.

Introduced in 1972 by Niles Eldredge and Stephen Gould as a description of the pattern in the fossil record, punctuated equilibrium centers on the ideas of stasis and sudden appearance. The major vehicle of evolutionary change becomes speciation, a process which gives rise to new species. Eldredge and Gould suggested that where there is lots of speciation, there should be lots of morphological differences. Where there is little speciation, there will be few morphological differences. Morphological change becomes associated with speciation.

If morphological change is supposed to be associated with speciation, then groups of organisms that contain large numbers of species should also display large morphological differences within the group. But there are numerous examples of specific groups of related organisms that contain large numbers of species, like the minnows *(Notropis)*, which show very little morphological divergence. This is exactly the opposite of the prediction. Sunfishes *(Lepomis)*, however, a group with relatively few species, show just as much, if not more, morphological divergence as the minnows. This is another contradiction of punctuated equilibrium, because here there is little speciation but a lot of differences.

An additional tricky aspect of the claims of punctuated equilibrium is that a new species of fossil can only be recognized because of observable differences, usually in the skeletal structure. Biological species, however, are designated by many criteria (chromosome structure, and so on) that cannot be detected in a fossil. Therefore, trying to extend a paleontological description of species and speciation will be very difficult.

What we see is that beyond punctuated equilibrium's ability to describe the fossil record, it is of little use to evolutionary biologists because they cannot imagine a way to make it work with real organisms. Gould and Eldredge admitted as much in their review of punctuated equilibrium's progress in the journal, *Nature,* when they lamented: "But continuing unhappiness, justified this time, focuses upon claims that speciation causes significant morphological change, for no validation of such a position has emerged."[5]

In addition, punctuationalists offer no mechanisms for arriving at new genetic information. No theory of evolutionary change is complete without some workable mechanism for generating new genetic information. There appears to be a general lack of appreciation as to what a mutation is, and what its effects on the organism may be. Discussions of regulatory and developmental mutations are carried out with no regard to the overwhelmingly destructive effect such mutations produce compared to mutations in structural genes. Developmental mutations can cripple an organism or even lead to its death. Thus, punctuated equilibrium raises more questions than it answers.

Another Alternative

As I have tried to point out, the two major competing models of evolutionary change are far from accepted facts of nature. Both have serious problems from which, some say, they may never be able to recover. However, if we sit back and view the evidence as a whole, a totally different perspective is possible.

First, virtually all taxonomic levels, even species, appear abruptly in the fossil record. This, it will be remembered, is one of the sharper criticisms of neo-Darwinism and one of the two cornerstones of punctuated equilibrium. It is relevant not only that the various levels of taxa appear abruptly but also that alongside the higher taxonomic levels there are unique adaptations. This is the key. Unique and highly specialized adaptations usually, if not always, appear fully formed in the fossil record. The origin of the different types of invertebrate animals such as the sponges, mollusks, echinoderms like the starfish, arthropods like crustaceans, and others all appear suddenly, without ancestors, in the Cambrian period.

Second, there is the steady maintenance of the basic body plan of the organism through time. One need only think of the living fossils from paleontology and of bacteria and the Drosophila fruit flies from genetics. The basic body plan does not change, whether analyzed through time in the fossil record or through mutations in the laboratory. Animal and plant breeders, through artificial selection, have reinforced this conclusion. There is much variation, but it can be manipulated only to a point.

Third, we found that in the few cases where organisms have adapted to new environments, it has predominantly happened through very ordinary processes using genetic variations that were probably always present in the species. Mutations, when they do play a role, produce defective organisms that survive and thrive only in unusual and unique environments. The chances of mutants outcompeting normal organisms in the wild are minute.

Fourth, we see the apparent inability of mutations truly to contribute to the origin of new structures. The theory of gene duplication in its present form is unable to account for the origin of new genetic information—a must for any theory of evolutionary mechanism.

Fifth, we can observe the amazing complexity and integration of the genetic machinery in every living cell. What we do know of the genetic machinery is impressive; what we have yet to learn staggers the imagination. How could mutation, selection, and speciation ever hope to improve or change the machinery in any substantial way? The cell poses an even bigger problem. The molecular workings of cilia, electron transport, protein synthesis, cellular targeting, and so on are simply astounding.[6]

The sixth and final element involves the big picture. Ecosystems themselves are a marvelous balance of complexity and integration. Energy flow or biomass flow through an ecosystem is as complicated as any biochemical pathway or genetic regulatory scheme. At the center of all this is the wondrous fit of an organism to its own peculiar environment. In the time before Darwin, this wondrous fit was considered evidence of a Supreme Designer.

The Natural Limits to Biological Change

Has Darwin's theory of natural selection really shown intelligent design in nature to be unreasonable? Since evolutionary mechanisms fail to be convincing, might biological change be a limited affair? Could the limits of biological change arise from the very nature of the genetic code itself, the unique set of structural and regulatory genes present in various groups of organisms and the tight organization and coadapted nature of the entire genome? I believe there are limits to biological change and that the structure and function of the genetic machinery set these limits.

Intelligent design is not a new concept. It's been around for centuries. Intelligent design, however, is today taking on a more sophisticated form. As knowledge of informational codes and information theory grows, the possibility of making predictions of the intricacy of the DNA informational code becomes more realistic. If DNA requires intelligent preprogramming, the signs should be unmistakable.

The mark of intelligence is not exactly hard to discern. We speak of the genetic code, DNA transcribed into RNA, RNA translated into protein. These are language terms. They are used not just because they are convenient, but because they accurately describe what is going on in the cell. There is a transfer of information. I believe that an application of information theory to the field of genetics will yield a comprehensible theory of limited biological change.

This is wholly reasonable because information theory concerns itself statistically with the essential characteristics of information and how that information is accurately transmitted or communicated. DNA is an informational code, so the connection is readily apparent. The overwhelming conclusion is that information does not and cannot arise spontaneously by mechanistic processes. Intelligence appears to be a necessity in the origin of any informational code, including the genetic code, no matter how much time is given.[7]

More directly, though, our concern is with what happens after the code is in place. Could intelligence be required for the first cell but not afterward? To answer that, we must look at the informational content of DNA a little more closely. Language involves two fundamental principles similar to the expression of genetic information. First, there is a finite set of words that is the essential content. In organisms, this is comparable to structural genes. Second, the rules of grammar provide for the richness of expression using the finite set of words. In organisms, these rules or programs consist of the regulatory and developmental mechanisms. In human language, with a finite set of words and a set of rules, the variety of expression goes on and on. It is conceivable, therefore, that different groups of organisms, maybe bats and whales, for example, are characterized by different regulatory mechanisms—that is, different developmental programs.

There is growing interest in a biological theory of intelligent design around the world. While many still vigorously oppose all such ideas, there is a much greater openness than ever before. Philosophers, mathematicians, chemists, engineers, and biologists are willing to suggest, even demand, that a more rigorous study of intelligent design in relation to biological organisms be pursued. A renaissance may be around the corner.[8]

Confirming New Data

It was known ten years ago that much of the information for the early stages of development were contained in the cytoplasm or the cell membrane. This has since been rigorously confirmed. There is information, therefore, that is possibly not contained in the nucleus. So our emphasis on the genetic material was a little too strong. There is at least another source of information to consider. This seems to imply that, in order to change the body plan, changes must be coordinated in perhaps two unrelated sources of information in the embryo. This would make a change in the developmental pathway even more difficult to achieve.[9]

Michael Denton's book, *Evolution: A Theory in Crisis,*[10] reveals that development through the earliest embryonic stages is vastly different in amphibians, reptiles, and mammals. Supposedly, similar early structures arise from nonsimilar structures and pathways in the embryo. This bears witness to our contention that unique developmental pathways would separate the basic types, even when the structures are thought to be homologous. The complexity of living things continues to astound the imagination. Michael Behe has introduced the term *irreducible complexity*. Irreducibly complex systems are systems which must have all molecular components present in order to be functional. He used the molecular machinery of cilia as an example. Cilia contain numerous molecular components, such as the proteins nexin, dynein, and microtubules that all need to be present if a cilium is to perform at all. Cilia cannot arise step-by-step in natural selection.

But perhaps the most gratifying confirmation of our ideas came about recently in the publication of a book edited by J. P. Moreland, *The Creation Hypothesis*. A chapter on the origin of human language contains this passage on the complexities of the genetic language.

> In order for any organism to be what it is, its genetic program (DNA) must specify what sort of organism it will be and, within surprisingly narrow limits, what specific characteristics it will assume. Such limits, innately determined, apply as much to a human being or to a Rhesus monkey as to a special variety of fruit fly or yeast or bacterium.[11]

Later, after discussing the cascade of information from DNA to protein, it concludes:

> The whole cascading network of relationships must be specified within rather

narrowly defined limits in order for any organism whatever to be a viable possibility. Moreover, the problem of biogenesis and the origin of human language capacity are linked at their basis by more than just a remarkable analogy. It turns out that the human genome must include the essential characteristics of the entire conceptual system that we find manifested in the great variety of languages and their uses, but within rather narrow limits, by human beings throughout the world.[12]

The use of such phrases as "narrowly defined limits" and "great variety" applying to both human languages and the information content of DNA is promising. If languages require intelligent preprogramming, then so does the genetic code.

It is difficult for me to imagine that honest men and women could study the immense complexities of even the "simplest" creatures and not marvel, or better yet worship, at the feet of their Creator.

4

Evolution's Big Bang
Ray Bohlin

The impish Calvin, from the now defunct daily comic strip "Calvin and Hobbes," once offered to rename the big bang hypothesis the "Horrendous Space Kablooie!" Most of us have heard at some point of cosmology's preferred explanation for the origin of the universe, the big bang hypothesis. The big bang of cosmology describes a powerful explosion that eventually resulted in the universe as we see it today. But a recent issue of *Time* magazine (December 4, 1995)[1] heralded a new big bang, a big bang of biological evolution previously known as the Cambrian explosion. And just as some draw theistic conclusions from cosmology's big bang, so it is possible to draw theistic conclusions from what is now being called evolution's big bang.

What is evolution's big bang? The cover of this issue of *Time* declared: "New discoveries show that life as we know it began in an amazing biological frenzy that changed the planet almost overnight." A subheading proclaimed, "For billions of years, simple creatures like plankton, bacteria, and algae ruled the earth. Then, suddenly, life got very complicated."[2]

The standard evolutionary story describes an earth

bombarded by meteorites from its origin 4.5 billion years ago until almost 3.8 billion years ago. In only 100 million years, the first life evolved following the cessation of this celestial onslaught. This, in and of itself, is a huge evolutionary hurdle without explanation. For the next 3 billion years, little else but single-celled life-forms ruled the planet. Then suddenly, in the Cambrian geological period, the earth became populated with a huge diversity of complex multicellular life-forms. This has always looked suspiciously like some form of creation event, and paleontologists frequently seemed rather embarrassed by the reality of the Cambrian explosion.

So, where is the documentation for the long history of the evolution of these creatures? The usual answer is that the necessary fossil layers prior to the Cambrian period have not been discovered yet. The fossils are just missing! This, after all, was Darwin's excuse, and many evolutionists after him have followed suit. Well, recent discoveries from Canada, Greenland, China, Siberia, and Namibia document quite clearly that this period of biological creativity occurred in a geological instant virtually all around the globe. So, the usual excuse no longer holds water. While evolutionists are not exactly being swept away by a creationist wave, they are being forced to ask tough questions concerning the nature of evolutionary change. Darwin did not envision a major evolutionary change happening this fast. Darwinism has always been characterized by a slow gradual change that is imperceptible in our time frame. Major evolutionary change was only visible as we looked to the fossils to reveal the number and type of intermediates between species and major groups. But the Cambrian explosion is anything but gradual, and identifiable intermediates are totally absent. Where are the ancestors? What conditions could have prompted this frenzy of creativity? Is there some form of unknowable evolutionary mechanism at work? I think you will find the evolutionary community's answers to be quite revealing.

How Fast Is Fast?

Anomalocaris! Ottoia! Wiwaxia! Hallucigenia! Opabinia! If these names are unfamiliar to you, well, they should be. They have only become familiar to paleontologists over the last twenty years. Paleontologists are those scientists who study the fossils embedded in ancient layers of rock. And this strange list represents a group of animals from the Cambrian period, a period that is only now being appreciated. These animals supposedly lived over 500 million years ago. They not only possess strange sounding names, they are strange looking! So strange and different are they that most are contained in phyla of which they are the only example and which no longer exist.

And just what are phyla? Well, if you remember high-school biology, *phyla* is actually the plural form of *phylum,* a Latin term designating a large category of biological classification. The largest category of classification is the kingdom. We all know about the animal and plant kingdoms. Well, phylum is the next category below kingdom. The animal kingdom consists of such well-known phyla as the mollusks, which contains clams, oysters, and snails. Another commonly known phylum is the annelids, to which belong earthworms. The largest of all the phyla is the arthropods. Arthropods range from insects to millipedes to spiders to shrimp. We are placed in the chordate phylum along with all other vertebrates—fish, amphibians, reptiles, birds, and other mammals. Representatives from different phyla are very different creatures. There is not much in common in a human, a mosquito, an earthworm, and a clam. They are all so different that evolutionists have assumed it must have taken tens of millions of years for them to evolve from one common ancestor.

Yet, here is the real puzzle of the Cambrian explosion for the theory of evolution. All known phyla, with the exception of one, first appeared in the Cambrian period. There are no ancestors. There are no intermediates. Fossil experts used to think that the Cambrian period lasted 75 million years, but even that seemed to be a pretty short time for all this evolutionary change. Eventually, it was shortened to 30 million years. As if that wasn't bad enough, recently the time frame for the real work of bringing all these different creatures into existence was limited to the first 5 to 10 million years of the Cambrian period. That is extraordinarily fast! Harvard's Stephen Jay Gould says, "Fast is now a lot faster than we thought, and that is extraordinarily interesting."[3] What an understatement! "Extraordinarily impossible" might be a better phrase!

Geologist Samuel Bowring says, "We now know how fast fast is. And what I like to ask my biologist friends is, How fast can evolution get before you start feeling uncomfortable?"[4] I would love to ask Bowring just what he meant by that question. It's almost as if he is recognizing that current evolutionary mechanisms can't possibly act that fast. Possible answers to that dilemma are only creating more questions—questions that evolutionists may never be able to answer.

How Could the Cambrian Explosion Occur?

Charles Darwin proposed an evolutionary process that was slow and gradual. This formulation has remained the mainstay of evolutionary explanations for over one hundred years. Today, one of the many reasons for a rethinking of this gradual, snail-like pace has been the intricate complexity of living things. In the years before Darwin, the marvelous fit of an organism to its environment was considered the chief evidence of a Supreme Designer.[5] Darwin supposedly showed another and better way—natural selection. But if organisms were so finely tuned to their environment, so wonderfully adapted to their particular niche, how and why would they change? If they were to change at all over time, the change would have to be very gradual so as not to upset the delicate balance between the organism and its environment.

This notion of the gradualness of the evolutionary process was reinforced by the discovery of DNA and the genetic code. DNA operates as an informational code for the development of an organism from a single cell to an adult and also regulates all the chemical processes that go on in cells. Mutations or mistakes in the code had to have very minor effects. The blueprint would be very sensitive to disruption. The small changes brought about by mutations would have to be cumulative over very long periods of time to bring about significant evolutionary changes.

This necessity of gradualism explains the difficulty evolutionists have concerning the Cambrian explosion or evolution's big bang. How could animals as diverse as arthropods, mollusks, jellyfish, and even primitive vertebrates all appear within a time span of only 5 to 10 million years with no ancestors and no intermediates? (True fish-like vertebrates have now been documented from Cambrian strata in China.)[6] Evolution just doesn't work this way. Fossil experts and biologists are only beginning to wrestle with this thorny dilemma. Some think that genes which control the process of development from a fertilized egg to an adult, the so-called Hox genes, may have reached a critical mass that led to an explosion of complexity. Some of the simplest multicelled organisms like the jellyfish only have three Hox genes, while insects have eight, and some not-quite vertebrates have ten. Critical mass may be a real phenomena in physics, but biological processes rarely, if ever, work that way. Besides, that doesn't solve the important riddle of where the first Hox gene came from in the first place. Hox genes now appear to be only molecular switches for just about any developmental pathway. The same Hox gene can turn on the development of very different structures in different organisms.[7] Genetic information does not just spontaneously arise from random DNA sequences.

Other scientists think that a wholesale reorganization of all the genes must have also occurred along with the duplication of Hox genes to bring about change of this magnitude. But that only complicates the picture by requiring additional, simultaneous genetic mutations. This would have an enormous negative effect on an organism that was already adapted to its environment. How could it survive? It seems that the equivalent of a miracle would be required. But such things aren't allowed in evolution. To quote *Time* magazine again, "Of course, understanding what made the Cambrian explosion possible doesn't address the larger question of what made it happen so fast. Here scientists delicately slide across ice-thin data, suggesting scenarios that are based on intuition rather than solid evidence."[8]

Why Hasn't Such Rapid Change Ever Happened Again?

If this rapid explosion of diversity could occur before, why hasn't such drastic change ever happened in the 500 million years since? The same basic body plans that arose in the Cambrian period remain surprisingly constant. Apparently, the most significant biological changes in the history of the earth occurred in less than 10 million years and, for 500 million years afterward, this level of change never happened again. Why not? This may seem like a simple question, but it is far more complicated than it appears.

Many biologists think the answer must lie within the genetic structure of organisms. During the Cambrian period, new forms of life could readily appear because the genetic structure of organisms was relatively loose. Once all the body plans came into existence and were successful, then these same genetic structures became relatively inflexible in order to preserve what worked so well. In other words, there may be genetic built-in limits to change. Developmental biologist Rudolf Raff said, "There must be limits to change. After all we've had these same old body plans for half a billion years."[9] As mentioned earlier, Lane Lester and I coauthored a book in 1984 titled *The Natural Limits to Biological Change.*[10] Though the limits to change we proposed were tighter than those the evolution scientists are proposing, it is the same basic idea. We even suggested that these limits would be found in the genetic organization and regulatory programs that are already built in.

Some evolutionists have gone so far as to suggest that the mechanisms of evolution which operated in the Cambrian period were probably radically different. This raises the possibility that we may never be able to study these mechanisms because animals with the proper genetic structure no longer exist. We are left only with the products of the Cambrian explosion and none of the precursors. Speculation will therefore be wild and uncontrollable, since there will be no way to test these theories. Fossils leave no trace of their genetic organization. We may never know how this marvelous burst of creativity occurred. Sounds like evolutionists may be faced with the very same problems they accuse creationists of stumbling over: a process that was unique to the past, unobservable in any shape or form, and unrepeatable.

Stuart Kaufmann, a leader in complexity theory, places his faith in self-organizing systems that spontaneously give rise to order out of chaos—a sort of a naturalistic, impersonal self-creator. A supernatural Creator performs the same function with the added benefit of providing a source of intelligent design as well.

The Marvelous Evidence of Creation and Design, and the Role of Worldview

So often at Probe our focus is on some issue that has the opposing forces shaped by worldview. A worldview is a system of beliefs or a philosophy of life that helps us interpret the world around us. We often compare a person's worldview to a pair of glasses that brings everything into focus. Just as it is important for someone with impaired vision to have the right prescription glasses, so it is necessary for sin-impaired people to have the right worldview with which to make sense of the world of ideas around them.

Clearly, we believe that the Bible is the only means by which we can arrive at the right prescription or worldview. But three weeks after the *Time* article was published, some very interesting letters appeared from readers. These letters demonstrated the way different worldviews can affect evaluation of evidence. One *Time* magazine reader commented, "This report should end discussions about whether God created the earth. Now there is no way to deny the theory of evolution."[11] Another reader said, "It is great to see a national magazine put the factual evidence of evolution's vast, complex story out there for the lay public."[12] Now, before you go assuming that they surely hadn't read the same story I have been describing in these pages, listen to readers with a different perspective: "A more appropriate title for your article could have been 'Evolution's Big Bust.' One hundred and thirty-five years of Darwinism out the window just like that? What a poor excuse for the lack of transitional forms."[13] Another reader said, "This story read more like confirmation for Noah's Deluge than Darwin's theory of evolution."[14]

Well, they all read the same story. Many even quoted from the article. So, how can four people read the same information and come to such radically different conclusions? The difference is worldview. For those working within a naturalistic worldview, one which holds that God (if He exists at all) has no influence on the physical universe, some form of evolution must be true. Therefore, while the evidence of the Cambrian period may be perplexing, the fact that scientists are wrestling with it and offering some possible explanations is exciting and invigorating. However, I find that naturalistic thinkers are usually missing the big picture. By concentrating on the minutiae they often miss the clear possibility of intelligent design—precisely because they don't expect to find any.

A great example of this is a comment by Harvard's Stephen Jay Gould on the Cambrian creatures found in the Burgess Shale of Canada. Gould was trying to come up with a metaphor that would encapsulate the wonder and diversity of the Burgess Shale. This is what he came up with: "Imagine an organism built of a hundred basic features, with twenty possible forms per feature. The grab bag contains a hundred compartments, with twenty tokens in each. To make a new Burgess creature, the Great-Token-Stringer takes one token at random from each compartment and strings them together. Voila, the creature works—and you have nearly as many successful experiments as a musical scale can build catchy tunes."[15]

Sounds like a marvelous description of a Creator to me, but perhaps only if you allow yourself to think outside philosophical naturalism from the start. Any musician will tell you that musical scales do not put together catchy tunes by themselves. A composer, a mind, is needed. Randomly choosing notes from a scale will only produce a cacophony of noise. Gould unwittingly points to the necessity of intelligent design to account for even the strangest of creatures.

5

Up a River Without a Paddle

A Darwinian View of Life

Ray Bohlin

A *River Out of Eden: A Darwinian View of Life* by Richard Dawkins is the fourth in a series being published by Basic Books entitled The Science Masters. This series is said to be "a global publishing venture consisting of original science books written by leading scientists." Purposing to "present cutting-edge ideas in a format that will enable a broad audience to attain scientific literacy," it is aimed at the nonspecialist.[1]

The first three releases were *The Last Three Minutes: Conjectures About the Ultimate End of the Universe* by Paul Davies, *The Origin of Humankind* by Richard Leakey, and *The Origin of the Universe* by John D. Barrow. These were followed by the contribution from Dawkins. A look at these books and at future contributors like Daniel Dennett, Jared Diamond, Stephen Jay Gould, Murray Gell-Mann, Lynn Margulis, and George C. Williams makes the endeavor look less like a scientific literacy series and more like an indoctrination in philosophical naturalism.

The exposition of a Darwinian view of life by Dawkins in *A River Out of Eden* certainly fits into the overt antitheistic category. The river referred to is a river of DNA, the true source of life, and the one molecule that must be understood if life itself is to be understood.

Metaphorically, Dawkins suggests that this river of DNA originally flowed as one river (one species) which eventually branched into two, three, four, and eventually millions of rivers. Each river is distinct from the others and no longer exchanges water with the others, just as species are isolated reproductively from other species and no longer exchange genes with each other. This metaphor allows Dawkins to explain both the common ancestry of all life along with the necessity of gradualism in the evolutionary process.

Dawkins also refers to this river of DNA as a digital river. Information contained in the DNA river is analogous to the digital information of languages and computers.

Surprisingly, Dawkins gives away the store in his first chapter. The digital analogy proves to be the death-knell for chance and necessity producing anything. In pressing home the digital analogy, Dawkins first uses probability to indicate that the code arose only once and that we all, therefore, are descended from a common ancestor: "The odds of arriving at the same 64:21 (64 codons: 21 amino acids) mapping twice by chance are less than one in a million million million million million. Yet the genetic code is, in fact, identical in all animals, plants and bacteria that have ever been looked at. All earthly living things are certainly descended from a single ancestor."[2]

What is fascinating about this statement is that Dawkins clearly believes it is reasonable to use probability to indicate that the code could not have arisen twice, but does not discuss the improbability of the code arising even once by chance. A curious omission! If one tried to challenge Dawkins in person, he would predictably fall back on the assumption of naturalism. Since we know only natural processes are available for the origin of anything, the genetic code must have somehow beaten the odds the first time.

African Eve

Dawkins next attempts to tell the story of the now famous "African Eve." African Eve embodies the idea that we are all descended from a single female, who probably lived in Africa, about two hundred thousand to one hundred thousand years ago. This conclusion originates from sequence data of the DNA contained in mitochondria.

Mitochondria are tiny little powerhouses that produce energy in each and every cell of our bodies. Just as our bodies contain many organs that perform different functions, the cell contains many organelles that also perform specific functions. The mitochondrion is an organelle whose task is to produce energy molecules the cell can use to accomplish its tasks.

However, mitochondria are also the only organelles to contain their own DNA. Certain proteins necessary to the function of mitochondria are coded for by the mitochondrial DNA and not by the nuclear DNA like every other protein in the cell. One other unique aspect of mitochondria is their maternal inheritance. That is, all the mitochondria in our bodies are descended from the ones we initially inherited from our mothers. The sperm injects only its DNA into the egg cell, not its mitochondria. Therefore, an analysis of mitochondrial DNA reveals maternal history only, uncluttered by the mixture of paternal DNA. That's why these studies only revealed an African Eve, though other recent studies claim to have followed DNA from the Y chromosome to indicate an ancient "Adam."

Now, scientists don't actually think they have uncovered proof of a real Adam and Eve. They only use the names as metaphors. But this action does reveal a shift in some evolutionists' minds to the idea that there is a single universal ancestor rather than a population of ancestors. This at least is closer to a biblical view rather than further away.

Finally, Dawkins makes his case for the reliability of these molecular phylogenies in general. Here he glosses over weaknesses in the theory and actually misrepresents the data. He says, "On the whole, the number of cytochrome c letter changes separating pairs of creatures is pretty much what we'd expect from previous ideas of the branching pattern of the evolutionary tree."[3] In other words, Dawkins thinks that the trees obtained from molecular sequences nearly matches the evolutionary trees already developed based on morphology. Later, when speaking of all molecular phylogenies performed on various sequences, he says, "They all yield pretty much the same family tree—which by the way, is rather good evidence, if evidence were needed, that the theory of evolution is true."[4]

Incredibly, besides implying that evidence is not really needed to prove evolution, Dawkins stumbles in trying to display confidence in the molecular data. What exactly does "pretty much" mean anyway? Inherent in that statement are the numerous contradictions that don't fit the predictions or the ambiguous holes in the general theory. But, why should I quibble; evidence isn't really needed anyway, is it?

Biochemist Michael Behe has shown that many of the assumptions of molecular evolution, such as the constant rate of nucleotide substitutions and our ability to predict which proteins evolve rapidly or slowly, do not mesh with the molecular evidence readily available.[5]

While this discussion contains the usual degree of arrogance from Dawkins, particularly in his disdain for the original account of Adam and Eve, it is somewhat less compelling or persuasive than is his usual style. He hedges his bets frequently and simply waives his hand at controversy. Unfortunately, the unwary reader may not pick this up.

Scoffing at Design

Dawkins then launches a full-scale assault on the argument from design. After presumably debunking arguments from the apparent design of mimicry (not perfect design, you know, just good enough), Dawkins states, "Never say, and never take seriously anybody who says, 'I cannot believe so-and-so could have evolved by gradual selection.' I have dubbed this fallacy 'the Argument from Personal Incredulity.'"[6]

To some degree I'm afraid that many creationists have given Dawkins and others an easy target. The statement, "I cannot believe. . . ." has been used many times by well-meaning creationists but is really not very defensible. It is not helpful to simply state that we can't believe something; we must elaborate the reasons why.

First, Dawkins levels the charge that much of what exists in nature is far from perfectly designed and is only "good enough." This, he claims, is to be expected of natural selection rather than a designer. A designer would design it right, while natural selection has to bumble and fumble its way to a solution. (Notice that Dawkins is drawing anti-theistic conclusions from natural history. Surely if one can draw negative religious conclusions from natural history, one ought to be able to legitimately draw positive religious conclusions without receiving the criticism that one is stepping outside the realm of science.)

To begin with, the lack of perfection in no way argues for or against a designer. I have always marveled at evolutionists who imply that if it isn't perfect, then nature did it. Just what is perfection? And how are we to be sure that the Creator agrees with our idea of a perfect design? We might not have a correct perception of what a perfect design is. This is a classic case of creating God in our own image. The evolutionists are the ones guilty of erecting the straw-man argument in this instance. In addition, Dawkins fully admits that things work well enough for the task at hand. The Creator only commanded His creatures to be fruitful and multiply, not necessarily to be perfectly designed wonders (humanly speaking). Romans 1:18–20 indicates that there is sufficient evidence if you investigate thoroughly.

Dawkins further closes off criticism by declaring that "there will be times when it is hard to think of what the gradual intermediates may have been. These will be challenges to our ingenuity, but if our ingenuity fails, so much the worse for our ingenuity."[7] So if explanations fail us, the fault is not with the evolutionary process, but with our limited thinking. How convenient that the evolutionary process is so unfalsifiable in this crucial area. But after all, he implies, this is science, and intelligent design is not! Dawkins tries to create a climate where evolutionary explanations are beyond criticism.

Dawkins concludes the chapter with a discussion on the evolution of the honeybee waggle dance. It is filled with probabilistic statements like, "The suggestion is that. . . . Perhaps the dance is a kind of. . . . It is not difficult to imagine. . . . Nobody knows why this happens, but it does. . . . It probably provided the necessary. . . ." Yet at the end, Dawkins proclaims, "Meanwhile, we have found a plausible series of graded intermediates by which the modern bee dance could have been evolved from simpler beginnings. The story as I have told it . . . may not be the right one. But something a bit like it surely did happen."[8]

Again, we know "it happened" only because any other explanation has been disallowed by definition, not by the evidence.

God's Utility Function

Dawkins concludes his attack on design, with a more philosophical discussion, which he calls "God's Utility Function." He begins with a discussion of the ubiquitous presence of "cruelty" in nature, even mentioning Darwin's loss of faith in the face of this reality. Of course, his answer is that nature is neither cruel nor kind—it's just indifferent.

But a curious admission ensues from his discussion. He says, "We humans have purpose on the brain."[9] Dawkins just drops that in to help him put down his fellow humans in his usual arrogant style. But I immediately asked myself, Where does this "purpose on the brain" stuff come from in a purely indifferent, chance and necessity universe? The rest of nature certainly seems indifferent. Why is it that man (within an evolutionary worldview) has "purpose on the brain"? In his attempt to be cute, Dawkins has asked an important question: Why *is* man unique in this respect?

As Christians, we recognize God as a purposeful being; therefore, if we are made in His image, we will be purposeful beings also. It is natural for us to ask "why" questions. No doubt, if pressed, evolutionists will dream up some selective or adaptive advantage for this trait. But this, as usual, would only be hindsight, based on an evolutionary worldview. There would be no data to back it up.

At the chapter's end, Dawkins returns to his initial topic. "So long as DNA is passed on, it does not matter who or what gets hurt in the process. . . . But Nature is neither kind nor unkind. . . . Nature is not interested one way or another in suffering, unless it affects the survival of DNA."[10] Even Dawkins admits that this is not a recipe for happiness. The problem of evil rears its head. Dawkins's simple answer is that there is no "problem" of evil. Nature just *is*.

He recounts a story from the British papers of a school bus crash with numerous fatalities and reports a Catholic priest's inadequate response to the inevitable "why" question. The priest had indicated that we really don't know why God would allow such things, but that these events at least confirm that we live in a world of real values —both positive and negative. "If the universe were just electrons, there would be no problem of evil or suffering," the priest said. Dawkins retorts that meaningless tragedies like this are what we expect from a universe composed only of electrons and selfish genes. Naturalism wins, you see, because naturalism predicts such events, whereas theism has to struggle to make sense of them.

However, this is also what we expect in a fallen world. Evolutionary writers rarely recognize this clear biblical theme. The world as we know it is not the way God intended His creation to be. What *is* unexpected in an evolutionary world are people shaped by *uncaring* natural selection who *care* about evil and suffering at all. Why are we not as indifferent as zebras?

In making his point, Dawkins says that the amount of suffering in the natural world is beyond all "decent" contemplation. Where does decency come from? He calls the bus crash a "terrible" story. Why is this so terrible if it is all meaningless? Clearly, Dawkins cannot live within the boundaries of his own worldview. He struggles to put moralistic tones on an event he is trying to tell us has no moral consequences, or, indeed, in a universe where there is no true morality!

We do see purpose, and we fret over suffering and evil, because we are created in the image of a God who has the same characteristics. There are aspects of our humanity that can not be explained by mutation and natural selection. Dawkins must *try* to explain them, because his naturalistic worldview leaves him no choice.

Are We Alone?

Dawkins closes his book with a chapter on the origin of life and a discussion on the possibilities of life elsewhere in the universe. This chapter is a disappointment because there is very little to say. To be sure, it is filled with the usual Dawkins arrogance and leaps of naturalistic logic, but there is no real conclusion—just the possibility of contacting whatever other life may be out there.

Dawkins begins by defining life as a replication bomb. Just as some stars eventually explode into supernovas, so some stars explode with information in the form of life—life that may eventually send radio messages or actual lifeforms out into space. Dawkins admits that ours is the only example of a replication bomb we know of, so it is difficult to generalize about the overall sequence of events between the time when life first appears and the time when it sends out information into space—but he does it anyway.

While we can clearly distinguish between random and intelligent radio messages, Dawkins is unable even to ask that question of the origin of the information-rich DNA code. He takes a few pages to evoke wonder from the reader by documenting the difficult barriers that had to be crossed. I suppose, then, his answer would be, "We do not know exactly what the original critical event, the initiation of self-replication, looked like, but we can infer what kind of an event it must have been. It began as a chemical event."[11] This inference is drawn not from chemical, geological, or biological data—because the real data contradicts such a notion.[12] His conclusion is an assumption derived from his naturalistic worldview. It was a chemical event because that is all that is allowed. Creation is excluded by definition, not by evidence. While chemical evolution may be difficult, we are assured that it happened!

The book closes with a discussion of the Ten Thresholds that must be crossed for a civilization of our type to exist. Along the way, Dawkins continues to overreach the evidence and make assumptions based on naturalism without the slightest thought that his scenario may be false or, at least, very wide of the mark.

All along the way Dawkins tries to amaze us with both the necessity and the complexity of each threshold but fails miserably to explain how each jump could have been accomplished. He depends totally on the explanatory power of natural selection for whatever transition is needed. It is just a matter of time.

But, of course, this begs the question. Dawkins perfects this art for 161 pages. Despite the smoke and mirrors, Richard Dawkins is still trying to travel up his river of DNA in a canoe without a paddle. It just won't work. While many of his explanations and ruminations require careful reading by creationists (he is not stupid and writes well), I have tried to point out his inconsistencies, assumptions, and poor logic.

What bothers me most is that *A River Out of Eden* is intended as a popular book. Dawkins's wit and dogmatism will convince and influence many. Because of this, I found it frustrating and sometimes maddening to read. Unfortunately, few will think their way through these pages and ask tough questions of the author. This is where the real danger lies. We must not only show others where he is wrong but also encourage them to discover errors on their own. We must help people to think.

Part 2

Intelligent Design

6

Contact

A Eulogy to Carl Sagan

Ray Bohlin

At the very beginning of the movie *Contact,* you might have noticed in the lower right corner of the screen a little dedication which read, "For Carl." This, of course, is Carl Sagan (1934–1996), the Cornell astronomer and science advocate, whose 1985 novel was the basis for the movie.[1] Sagan passed away in December 1996, before the movie was released. He had struggled for several years with a rare blood disorder.

The movie serves as a fitting eulogy for the most visible member of the scientific community within popular culture. The phrase "billions and billions," attributed to Sagan, has become a part of the public's lexicon of scientific phrases, even though Sagan never actually used the phrase in print or in any of his public broadcasts and appearances. Sagan used it self-effacingly as the title for his final book, published posthumously.

Many of us have heard of Carl Sagan, but we know very little about him. As a planetary astronomer, Sagan made significant contributions to the fields of chemical evolution, Martian topography, and Venusian meteorology. He also served as an official adviser to NASA on the *Mariner,*

Voyager, and *Viking* unmanned space missions. Carl Sagan coaxed the public and Congress for funds for space research and particularly for SETI, the Search for Extra-Terrestrial Intelligence.

Sagan was awarded the Peabody Award and an Emmy for his stunningly influential public television series, *Cosmos.* The accompanying book by the same title is the best-selling science book ever published in the English language.[2] He earned the Pulitzer Prize for his book *Dragons of Eden,* on the evolution of human intelligence, and numerous other awards and honorary degrees. He is the most widely read scientific author in the world, and upon awarding him their highest honor, the National Science Foundation heralded his gifts to mankind as "infinite."

The main character of *Contact,* Ellie Arroway, played by Jodie Foster, portrays Sagan's life in miniature. While not sharing Sagan's awards and rapport with the public, Ellie Arroway is a brilliant, driven, and self-reliant young astronomer obsessed with SETI. Dr. Arroway endures scorn and ridicule from the public and the scientific community for dedicating herself to the discovery of signs of extraterrestrial life, just as Sagan did in his lifetime. Arroway, like Sagan, confronted with the demons of superstition, fundamentalism, and scientific jealousy, fights back with reason, sarcastic wit, and sheer perseverance.

Arroway shares Sagan's views on the need for a rational, nonreligious grasp of reality to solve our problems; his hope for an extraterrestrial savior to rescue us from our technological adolescence; his wonder at the beauty of the cosmos; and his understanding of our species as a curious, brave, precious accident of the universe. What is paradoxical about *Contact* is not the conflict between faith and reason, but *who* is forced to rely on faith and experience instead of evidence. Following Ellie's trip through the galaxy and her conversation with an alien, she returns with no documentation. What actually was an eighteen-hour experience for Ellie appeared to be an uneventful few seconds for everyone else. She must ask a congressional panel to accept her account of events on *faith*. If you were paying close attention as the film wound down, however, you could discover that a paradox is apparent. Ellie's data instruments have recorded a full eighteen hours—not a few seconds— of static. There was empirical evidence of her experience after all, but it was withheld from Ellie by apprehensive government officials. Scientific validation once again highlights Sagan's conviction that science is humanity's only reliable tool in the discovery of truth, and that faith only covers up our fears and stifles our search for answers.

Contact is a must-see film for those who wish to comprehend and knowingly confront our culture's hostility toward faith that relies on revelation.

The Paradox of Sagan's Views of Religion

One of the most perplexing aspects of the movie *Contact* is the seemingly confusing portrayal of religion. The confusion, I believe, is only superficial. If you reflect on how the different characters are presented, science remains on its pedestal, and traditional religion is discarded as irrelevant at best and dangerous at worst.

Sagan's disdain for traditional religion is clear from the beginning. Flashbacks from Ellie's childhood in the early part of the movie lay the groundwork for her rational rejection of traditional Christianity. In the novel, Ellie's father is portrayed as skeptical of revealed religion; he views the Bible as "half barbarian history and half fairy tales."[3] In the movie, Ellie admits to Palmer Joss that her father was asked to keep her home from Sunday school because she asked too many questions that could not be answered, such as, "Where did Cain get his wife?" Although this and other objections offered in the novel are easily answered, they are left unchallenged as apparently sturdy nails in the Bible's coffin.

When Ellie's father dies in the movie, the clergyman offers harsh and uncaring words—that some things are hard to understand, that we aren't meant to understand them anyway, and that we just have to accept them as God's will. This deliberately presents the God of the Bible as unknowable and cruelly inscrutable, demanding only blind acceptance. Ellie's response to the minister is to berate herself for not leaving extra medicine where her father could have reached it in an emergency. Self-reliance and analytical thinking easily outcompete the minister's feeble lecture. In a conversation with Palmer Joss, Ellie confidently asserts that we created God so we wouldn't feel so small and alone. He's just an emotional crutch.

Two other characters in the film outline Sagan's view of the modern evangelical right. The long-haired preaching zealot is portrayed as a dangerous man, out of control and out of touch with reality. He later borrows a trick from Muslim fundamentalists by sacrificing himself in an attempt to derail the building of the travel machine. Richard Rank, the presidential advisor, represents that portion of the religious right that hungers and thirsts, not for righteousness, but for political power. At a cabinet meeting Rank offers sanctimonious drivel about science intruding into areas of faith and the message being morally ambiguous. If his remarks made you cringe with anger, they were supposed to.

And then there is Palmer Joss, the enigmatic, amoral

former priest. Palmer Joss's New Age religion sees truth as relative and the real issue as oppression. Joss has no quibble with the conclusions of science, just its attempts to overstep its boundaries and rule our lives. His knowledge of God is limited to an experience on which he does not elaborate, one that intellect cannot touch. Perhaps the attraction between Joss and Arroway is the challenge they represent to each other. Joss's religion is at least scientifically informed and therefore intriguing to Ellie, and Ellie is scorned by the same scientific establishment that Joss distrusts. A match made in Hollywood.

Sagan left no room for a faith that does not embrace the conclusions of scientific materialism. This needs to be kept in mind when Joss challenges Ellie about her belief in God during the hearings. When the other multinational members speak up in defense of Joss's question, it is clear they are only referring to some politically correct supreme being, not the God of Abraham, Isaac, and Jacob.

Sagan's Extraterrestrial Hope

Even in a scientifically sophisticated film such as Carl Sagan's *Contact,* we run into our culture's preoccupation with life beyond our planet. Though Carl Sagan spent some of his time combating the UFO crazies, he nevertheless held out a hope that there are civilizations out there waiting to discover us, or we them. Where did this conviction come from? For a scientific materialist and humanist like Carl Sagan, this confidence comes from two sources. First is the notion that if life evolved here, it is presumptuous of us to think that we are alone. Certainly life has evolved elsewhere! Second is Sagan's and others' fear that our species sits on the brink of self-destruction and that we need some outside help to overcome our predicament.

In a conversation with Palmer Joss, Ellie Arroway gives a calculation of sorts to explain her confidence that life has evolved elsewhere. She looks up into the plethora of stars in the nighttime sky and says, "If just one in a million of those stars has planets, and if only one in a million of those has life, and if just one in a million of those has intelligent life, then there are millions of civilizations out there." It is a little surprising that a film of such high caliber would get this wrong. If you take each of those probabilities and multiply them together, that's one in a million million million, or a billion billion, or in scientific notation, ten to the eighteenth power. Current estimates suggest that the stars number approximately ten to the twenty-second power. That would technically leave only ten thousand civilizations in the universe, not millions. That would mean that we are alone, at least in our own galaxy.

The Christian astronomer Hugh Ross estimated the probability of all the necessary conditions for life occurring by natural processes. Ross concluded that if all we have to depend on are physical and chemical processes, then we are alone in the universe. Life could have evolved nowhere else. Even the biochemical complexities of living cells are revealing that life requires intelligence (see chapter 9 on *Darwin's Black Box*). Sagan's confidence that life is super-abundant in the universe is grossly unsupported.

The second reason for Sagan's hope of other civilizations was expressed well by Ellie Arroway. An international panel, assigned the task of choosing the one individual who would enter the machine and perhaps visit the alien civilization, asked the candidates what one question they would pose when they got there. Ellie said she would want to know how the alien civilization survived their technological adolescence without destroying themselves. In the opening scene of Sagan's *Cosmos* television series he remarked that our species was "young and curious and brave; it showed much promise."[4] Sagan had been a tireless supporter of nuclear disarmament. He truly feared that we would destroy ourselves before we reached our full potential. Couple this fear with the conviction that there is no God, and we see why Sagan's only source of hope for salvation from ourselves was another, more advanced civilization that could give us some pointers for survival.

This confidence, that aliens who could contact us would necessarily be more advanced, is not unreasonable. If they had the technology to contact us purposefully, and we could not contact them, then their technology would have to be beyond ours. What is never explained, however, even though it is raised in the movie, is why we would expect this alien culture to be benevolent. This hope reflects more on Carl Sagan's optimistic cosmic humanism than any scientific reality. It is just as likely, if not more likely, that an alien civilization would be more of the variety portrayed in the movie *Independence Day*.

Who Will Save Us, God or Aliens?

The movie *Contact* depicts a more realistic scenario for a first encounter with an alien civilization than, say, *Men in Black*. A radio signal is received from space, broadcast at a frequency equal to the value of hydrogen times *pi*. It gets earth's attention by counting the prime numbers from 1 to 101 in sequence. The message has come from the star Vega, twenty-six light years away. It is eventually decoded and is found to contain plans for the construction of a machine for one person to travel out into the galaxy. Ellie

Arroway, the young astronomer who found the message, eventually boards the machine and travels out into space for a close encounter of a supposedly more realistic kind.

A very tantalizing line is repeated three times in the course of the film. When Ellie Arroway, as a child, asks her father if there are any life-forms out in the universe, he says that if there aren't, it would be an awful waste of space. Palmer Joss repeats the line to an adult Ellie as they engage in conversation under a starry sky in Puerto Rico. It is a poignant scene. Ellie is clearly stunned as she recalls her father saying the same thing. Ellie, herself, repeats the phrase at the end of the film as she addresses a group of school children and is asked if there is life out in space.

Sagan has drawn a bead on the argument for the existence of God from design, or the teleological argument. Waste implies misdirected design. If the universe was created for us, and if we are alone, why does it have to be so big? Surely we could have survived quite well in a much smaller and more economical universe. But if you think about it, Scripture proclaims that the heavens declare the glory of God, not man (Ps. 19:1). Indeed, if the universe had been created only for our benefit, then it *would* be a waste of space. We don't deserve it. But if the main purpose of the universe is to glorify the splendid, eternal, all-powerful God, it could never be big enough.

Another interesting theme is the form that the alien takes. After Ellie travels through the galaxy, she arrives at a large docking space station. She is somehow transported to a beach, resembling the picture of Pensacola, Florida, she drew as a child. Eventually, a figure approaches. It seems to be her father. Actually, it is an alien appearing to her in the form of her father. He tells her that they thought this would make it easier for her.

It's fascinating that Sagan often argued that if God exists, He should make Himself plain. Why not a cross in the sky or a mathematical formula in the Bible? Why is everything so obscure? One answer from Philip Yancey's book, *Disappointment with God,* is that God did reveal Himself plainly to Israel during the Exodus and they still rebelled, and Jesus performed incredible miracles and still most rejected Him. God does not want to coerce our love. So isn't it interesting that in Sagan's own story, when a superior intelligence wants to make contact with us, it puts us in familiar surroundings, takes on our form, and speaks our language? If it appeared to us in its true form, we would be afraid. Isn't that precisely what the Father did for us in sending Jesus to live among us? It appears that Carl Sagan has unwittingly answered his own objection.

The Worldview of Carl Sagan

Carl Sagan begins his highly acclaimed public television series *Cosmos* with a grand overview of the universe and our place within it. With crashing surf in the background, Sagan declares, "The cosmos is all that is or ever was or ever will be."[5]

Sagan eloquently expresses his conviction that matter and energy are all that exist. He goes on to describe his awe and wonder. He describes a tingling in the spine. There is a catch in his voice as the greatest of mysteries is approached. With excitement, Sagan tells us our tiny planetary home, the earth, is lost somewhere between immensity and eternity, thus poignantly emphasizing our simultaneous value and insignificance.

In the movie *Contact,* Dr. Ellie Arroway expresses this awe and wonder at several points in the film. The most dramatic episode occurs during her galactic spaceflight when she sees the center of the galaxy. She is at a loss for words in the face of such beauty and humbly suggests that a poet may have been a better choice to send on the trip.

While this is all very moving, the emotion seems strangely misplaced and inappropriate. If the cosmos is indeed all there is or ever was or ever will be, why get excited? If we are lost between immensity and eternity, shouldn't our reaction be one of existential terror, not awe? Sagan borrows this excitement from a Christian worldview, where the heavens declare the glory of God. This *should* produce a tingle in the spine and a catch in the voice.

In the next to final scene in *Contact,* Ellie attempts to defend herself by finally admitting that she has no evidence of her trip through the galaxy. But she has been given something wonderful—a vision of the universe that tells us how tiny, insignificant, rare, and precious we are. In *Cosmos,* Sagan reflects that while we are a young, curious, and brave species, our place in the universe is to be compared to "a mote of dust that floats in the morning sky."[6]

How can we be tiny and insignificant and rare and precious all at the same time? Clearly Sagan cannot live consistently within his own worldview. His view of the universe dictates that all is meaningless chance and we are nothing special, yet he irrationally rejects the despair that logically follows, in favor of being curious, brave, rare, and precious.

As Sagan neared death, many around the world were praying for him. Though he was clearly an enemy of the faith, his closing sentences in the novel *Contact* indicated a belief in and a hope for an intelligence that antedates the universe. Might he see the whole truth before he passes into eternity? In his final book *Billions and Billions,* his wife Ann Druyan writes, "Contrary to the fantasies of fundamentalists, there was no deathbed conversion. . . . Even at this moment when anyone would be forgiven for turning away from the reality of our situation, Carl was unflinching."[7] In reflecting on the many cards and letters she received upon his death from people telling of the impact Sagan had on their lives, she writes, "These thoughts comfort me and lift me out of my heartache. They allow me to feel, without resorting to the supernatural, that Carl lives."[8]

Sadly, Carl does live, but not as she believes. Remember that enemies of the faith are lost and in need of a Savior. But even though they may be prayed for and witnessed to by colleagues up to the end, many, including Carl Sagan, will still defiantly die in their sins. It is a bitter, needless grief.

7

Are We Alone in the Universe?

Ray Bohlin

In August of 1996, there was great excitement in the media over an announcement by a group of scientists from NASA, proclaiming that evidence of life on Mars had been found. Their evidence, an alleged Martian meteorite, was shoved to center stage, and every news program from CNN to *Nightline* ran special interviews and video footage of the scientists and their prized specimen. President Clinton was so excited by the announcement that he praised the United States space program and took the opportunity to establish a bipartisan space summit headed by Vice President Al Gore to study the future of American space research. Hopefully, we were already doing that.

Clearly this announcement took the country by storm. Some of the scientists gushed embarrassingly over the significance of these findings. The media frenzy was prompted by the early release of an article from *Science,* the premier scientific journal in the United States. The article was due to be published the following week, but *Science* decided to release it early because it had already leaked out.

A group of scientists had studied a meteorite found in the ice of Antarctica. Previously it had been determined, by studying the gaseous content of glass-like components of the meteor, that this meteorite had originated on Mars.

The gas composition matched the atmosphere of Mars very closely. The conclusion seemed reasonable.

Next, they looked for evidence of life on and in the crevices of the meteor. They found two types of molecules that can form as a result of life processes—carbonates and complex molecules called polyaromatic hydrocarbons or PAHs. They also found shapes in the rock that resembled those of known microfossils on earth. Microfossils are fossils of one-celled organisms that are tricky to interpret.[1]

Obviously NASA scientists believed they had provided ample evidence to conclude that life once existed on Mars. However, as they readily acknowledged, the chemical signs could all be due to processes that have nothing to do with life. The supposed microfossils are at least ten times smaller than any such fossils found on earth. Other groups that studied this same meteorite concluded that either the temperature of the formation of the chemicals was far too high to allow life (over 700 degrees Centigrade), or that other chemical signals for life were absent.[2] William Schopf, a paleontologist from the University of California at Los Angeles, said, "I think it's very unlikely they have remnants of biological activity."[3] But if you read the concluding statement in the actual paper in *Science* you see a tentative position not evident in the press conference: "Although there are alternative explanations for each of these phenomena taken individually, when they are considered collectively, particularly in view of their spatial association, we conclude that they are evidence for primitive life on Mars."[4]

In plain English, the article was saying there are reasonable nonlife explanations for each of the evidences presented, but still we think they mean there is (was) life on Mars. The evidence *is* equivocal and was challenged by many other scientists, but the media did not report that as fully.

What Would Life on Mars Mean?

Because of the announcement, many people were encouraged in their belief that we are not alone in the universe. In fact, the signs for Martian life are far from certain and probably wrong—but if they were proved true, what would these results mean to evolutionists? Moreover, is there any reason for Christians to fear confirmation of life on Mars?

Let us assume, for the moment that the information from this Martian meteorite is legitimate evidence for life on Mars—that life, at some point in the past, actually existed on Mars. What does it mean?

For evolutionists, the evidence is perceived as confirmation that life can arise from nonlife by purely chemical processes. In addition, evolutionists draw the conclusion that life can evolve easily since it did so on two adjacent planets in the same solar system. Therefore, even though terrestrial origin-of-life research is at a standstill, such a discovery would seemingly confirm the notion that *some* chemical evolution scenario *must work*.

On the other hand, some have stated that if there is life on Mars, creationism has been dealt a death blow. They rationalize that since (1) we would now know that life can evolve other places, and (2) the Bible never speaks of life anywhere but on earth, the Bible is, therefore, unreliable. Besides, they reason, why would God create life on a planet with no humans? However, since the Bible is absolutely silent on the subject of extraterrestrial life, we can make no predictions about its possibility. God is certainly free to create life on planets other than earth if He chooses.

The real question is whether the proper conclusion to

the evidence found in the meteorite is, in fact, that life originated on Mars. The simple answer, inexplicably avoided by the media, is *no*! The most obvious answer to the possible discovery of life on Mars is that the so-called "Martian life" actually came from earth!

Think about it this way. The meteorite that was found is supposed to have existed on Mars previously. How did it get to earth? Well, it is hypothesized that a large meteorite crashed into Mars throwing up lots of debris into space, some of which found its way to earth and at least a few pieces of which were discovered by earthlings. If you are following along with me, you will now realize that the same scenario could have been played out in reverse to send terrestrial life to Mars.

Evolutionists suggest that the earth was under heavy meteor bombardment until at least 3.8 billion years ago—about the time they say life appeared on earth. Therefore, large meteorites reached the earth in great numbers when life was emerging. Christian astronomer Hugh Ross explains it this way: "Meteorites large enough to make a crater greater than 60 miles across will cause earth rocks to escape earth's gravity. Out of 1,000 such rocks ejected, 291 strike Venus, 20 go to Mercury, 17 hit Mars, 14 make it to Jupiter, and 1 goes all the way to Saturn. Traveling the distance with these rocks will be many varieties of earth life."[5]

Ross also documents that many forms of microscopic life are quite capable of surviving such a journey. All this is quite well known in the scientific community, but I have not seen it mentioned once in any public discussion. I believe the reason is that the possibility of life having evolved on Mars is too enticing to pass up.

The Improbability of Life Elsewhere in the Universe

Let's turn our attention to the amazing optimism of many who claim that the universe is teeming with life. No doubt it is fueled by the tremendous success of such science-fiction works as *Star Wars,* and *Star Trek,* which eloquently present the reasonableness of a universe full of intelligent life-forms.

Inherent in this optimism is the evolutionary assumption that if life evolved here, certainly we should not arrogantly suppose that life could not have evolved elsewhere in the universe. And if life in general exists in the universe, then, of course, there must be intelligent life out there as well.

This is the basic assumption of the SETI program, the Search for Extra-Terrestrial Intelligence. It is a program, now privately funded, that searches space for the first radio wave, among the millions of randomly generated radio waves, that would carry the mark of intelligence. But is such a hope realistic? Is there a justifiable reason for suspecting that planets suitable to life exist elsewhere in the universe?

Over the last two decades scientists have begun tabulating the many characteristics of our universe, galaxy, solar system, and planet that need to be finely tuned for life to exist. Christian astronomer and apologist Dr. Hugh Ross documents all these characteristics in his book *Creator and the Cosmos*[6] and he is constantly updating them. Ross documents twenty-six characteristics of the universe and thirty-three characteristics of our galaxy, solar system, and planet that are exactly the way they must be for life to exist.

Some examples include the size, temperature, and brightness of our sun; the size, chemical composition, and stable orbit of earth; the fact that we have one moon, not none or two or three; the distance of the earth from the sun; the tilt of the earth's axis; the speed of the earth's rotation; and the time it takes earth to orbit the sun. If any of these factors were different, even by a small percentage, the ability of earth to sustain life would be severely compromised. Recently it has been noted that even the presence of Jupiter and Saturn serve to stabilize the orbit of earth. Without these two large planets, located exactly where they are, the earth would be knocked out of its present near-circular orbit into an highly elliptical orbit, causing higher temperature differences between seasons and subjecting earth to greater meteor interference. Neither condition is hospitable to the continuing presence of life.

Ross has further calculated the probabilities of all these factors coming together by natural processes alone to be one in 10^{-53}, that's a decimal point followed by fifty-two zeroes and then a one. A very liberal estimate of how many planets there may be, though we have only documented eighteen, is 10^{22} or 10 billion trillion planets, one for every star in the universe. Combining these two probabilities tells us that there are 10^{-31} planets in the entire universe that could support life. Obviously this is far less than one. By natural processes alone, even *we* shouldn't be here—let alone some kind of alien life-form.

Unless God created life elsewhere, we are alone. For the materialistic evolutionist that is a frightening possibility. Just imagine a universe in which there is no God and no other intelligent life either. The sense of isolation and loneliness would be oppressive.

Problems with Chemical Evolution on Earth

The statistics given above show that we really are alone in the universe and that there is no hope of finding intelligent civilizations the way the television program *Star Trek* depicts. And while that means there is no one out there to threaten our survival, it also means there is no one out there to save us from our own mistakes.

This observation indicates why I believe the scientific community and the media became so excited about the possibilities of life on Mars. Efforts to determine how life could have evolved from nonliving matter have been so fraught with problems that the possibility of life elsewhere is extremely remote. But if it could be proved that life evolved elsewhere, then it would demonstrate that life can spring up easily, and that we just haven't found the right trick here on earth to prove it.

But is the evolution of life from nonliving chemicals really that impossible? The difficulties fall into three categories: the chemical problem, the thermodynamic problem, and the informational problem. These issues are presented comprehensively in a book by Thaxton, Bradley, and Olsen titled *The Mystery of Life's Origin*[7] and in a chapter by Bradley and Thaxton in the edited volume by J. P. Moreland, *The Creation Hypothesis.*[8]

Chemical problems are illustrated by the difficulty of synthesizing even the simplest building-block molecules necessary for life from inorganic precursors. Amino acids, sugars, and the bases for the important nucleotide molecules that make up DNA and RNA were all thought to be easily synthesized in an early earth atmosphere of ammonia, methane, water vapor, and hydrogen. But further experiments have shown this to be unrealistic. Ammonia and methane would have been short-lived in this atmosphere; the multiple energy sources available would have destroyed the necessary molecules, and water would have broken apart into hydrogen and oxygen. Oxygen was scrupulously avoided in all prebiotic scenarios because it would have poisoned all the necessary reactions.

Thermodynamic problems arise from the difficulty in assembling all these complex molecules that would have been floating around in some prebiotic soup into a highly organized and complex cell. To accomplish the task of achieving specified complexity (numerous different molecules arranged in a precise pattern) of life's molecules such as DNA and proteins, the availability of raw energy for millions of years is not enough. All systems where specified complexity is produced from simple components require an energy conversion mechanism to channel the energy in the right direction to accomplish the necessary work. Without photosynthesis, there is no such mechanism in the prebiotic earth. Since we are talking about the first cell, there could, as yet, be no photosynthesis.

The *informational problem* shows that there is no way to account for the origin of the genetic code, which is a language, without intelligent input. Informational codes require intelligent preprogramming. No evolutionary mechanism can accomplish this. Life requires intelligence.

So you can see why evolutionists would get excited about the possibility of finding evolved life elsewhere. It's because life is seemingly impossible to evolve here. So, if it did happen elsewhere, maybe our experiments are just missing something.

Independence Day, the Movie

In the movie *Independence Day,* an alien battle force swoops down on earth with the intention of destroying the human race, sucking the planet dry of all available resources, and then moving on to some other unlucky civilization in the galaxy. But those indomitable humans, aided by good old American ingenuity, outsmart the dull-witted aliens, and earth is saved. The story has been told many times, but perhaps never as well or never with such great special effects. The movie was a huge success.

But why are we continually fascinated by the possibility of alien cultures? The movie gave the clear impression that there must be great numbers of intelligent civilizations out there in the universe. This notion has become widely accepted in our culture.

Few recognize that the supposed existence of alien civilizations is based on evolutionary assumptions. The science fiction of *Star Trek* and *Star Wars* begins with evolution. As I've stated earlier, evolutionists simply rationalize that since life evolved here with no outside interference, the universe must be full of life. Astronomer Carl Sagan, after he had reviewed the so-called success of early earth chemical evolution experiments, put it this way: "Nothing in such experiments is unique to the earth. The initial gases, and the energy sources, are common throughout the Cosmos. Chemical reactions like those in our laboratory vessels may be responsible for the organic matter in interstellar space and the amino acids found in meteorites. Some similar chemistry must have occurred on a billion other worlds in the Milky Way Galaxy. The molecules of life fill the Cosmos."[9]

Sagan strongly suggests that the probabilities and chemistry of the universe dictate that life is ubiquitous in the galaxy. But as I stated earlier, the odds overwhelmingly dictate that our planet is the only one suitable for life in the universe, let alone our own galaxy. And the chemistry on earth also indicates that life is extremely hard to come by. The probability of life simply based on chance occurrences is admitted by many evolutionists to be remote indeed. Many are now suggesting that life is inevitable because there are as yet undiscovered laws of nature that automatically lead to complex life-forms. In other words, the deck of cards is fixed. Listen to Nobel Laureate and biochemist, Christian de Duve:

> We are being dealt thirteen spades not once but thousands of times in succession! This is utterly impossible, unless the deck is doctored. What this doctoring implies with respect to the assembly of the first cell is that most of the steps involved must have had a very high likelihood of taking place under the prevailing conditions. Make them even moderately improbable and the process must abort, however many times it is initiated, because of the very number of successive steps involved. In other words, contrary to Monod's affirmation, the universe was— and presumably still is—pregnant with life.[10]

The only problem with de Duve's suggestion is that we know of no natural processes that will lead automatically to the complexity of life. Everything we know of life leads to the opposite conclusion. Life is not a product of chance or necessity. Life is a product of intelligence.

Without divine interference, we are alone in the universe, and without Christ we are—and should be—terrified. The gospel is as relevant as ever.

8

Defeating Darwinism

Phillip Johnson Steals the Microphone

Rick Wade

I f you keep close tabs on the creation/evolution debate, you've probably already heard the name Phillip E. Johnson. If you're interested in seeing how one Christian is challenging the dogma of Darwinism, you'll want to know about this man.

Johnson is a law professor at the University of California, Berkeley. In the summer of 1997, InterVarsity Press published *Defeating Darwinism by Opening Minds,* Johnson's third book in his debate with naturalistic evolution.[1] His first book, *Darwin on Trial,* examined the scientific evidence for evolution and launched a series of lectures and debates across the United States and overseas, in universities and on radio and television.[2] His second book, *Reason in the Balance,* examined the influence of naturalism in the spheres of science, law, and education.[3] *Defeating Darwinism* brings his case to high school and early college-level students and their parents.

So, what prompted a law professor to take on the evolutionists? It seems that Johnson became aware of a significant difference between the way the theory of evolution is presented to the public and the way it's discussed among scientists. To the general public, evolution is presented as being settled with respect to the really important questions. Among scientists, however, there is still no consensus as to how evolution could have occurred. As another author said, evolution is a theory in crisis.[4] Professor Johnson studied the literature closely and concluded that what keeps the "evolution-as-fact" dogma alive is not scientific evidence at all, but rather a commitment to the philosophy of naturalism.

Naturalism is the belief that everything that exists is on the same basic level, that of nature. There is no God who created the universe, whether in six days or in 15 billion years.

One needs to be cautious here. Many scientists believe in God. However, the rule of the day in the laboratory and the classroom is a commitment to the philosophy of naturalism or at least to practical naturalism. Consequently, whether there is a God or not, no reference can be made to Him in the realm of scientific study.

Two reasons come to mind to explain why Johnson has received such a wide hearing in secular academia. First, he keeps the focus on evolution, *not* on a particular theory of creation. This is annoying to some evolutionists. But Johnson knows that as soon as he allows his views to be put under the spotlight, the debate will be over. Why? Because the evolutionists will immediately label his views as "religious," and he will be dismissed out of hand. Second, he is a legal scholar with years of experience in the logical analysis of evidence. He has the skill to carefully dissect the arguments of evolutionists, show their weaknesses, and reveal their unargued presuppositions.

Now let's take a closer look at Johnson's book *Defeating Darwinism*. We'll see how evolution gained dominance as a theory of origins, and we'll learn how Johnson exposes its *un*scientific foundations. I urge you to get a copy of this book even if science isn't your area, just to learn one way to engage our culture in the realm of ideas.

Where's the Beef?

In his new book, *Defeating Darwinism by Opening Minds,* Phillip Johnson seeks to help high school and college students and their parents evaluate the claims of Darwinism.

In his first book, *Darwin on Trial,* Johnson described the evidential problems with evolution in some detail. In *Defeating Darwinism,* he simply notes that possible transitional forms in the fossil record are very few in number and they are not found where fossil evidence is most plentiful. The problem, he says, is that textbooks and museums often present evidence in a way that implies there is more evidence available than there really is. As an example, Johnson points to an exhibit in San Francisco called the "Hard Facts Wall," which fills in gaps in the fossil record with imaginary ancestors. Says Johnson: "Visitors to the museum at first take the exhibit at face value; after I explain it to them, they are astonished that a reputable museum would commit such a deception. But the museum curators are not consciously dishonest; they are true believers who are just trying too hard to help the public get to the 'right' answer."[5]

Even though the physical evidence is not there, and there is no known mechanism for the transition from one type of organism to another, the scientific community clings to evolution as fact. The reasoning seems to be this: Since science studies the natural order, scientific theory must remain within naturalistic bounds. Since neo-Darwinism is the best naturalistic theory, it *must* be true.

This commitment extends beyond simply influencing scientific study; it is indoctrinated into students as the way things are. Johnson says that "when students ask intelligent questions like 'Is this stuff really true?' teachers are encouraged or required not to take the questions seriously."[6]

A fifteen-year-old high school student found out about the power of Darwinist orthodoxy when he challenged a requirement to watch a program on public television which promoted the "molecule to man" theory as fact. When school administrators showed an inclination to go along, the bottom fell out. Johnson stated, "The Darwinists . . . flooded the city's newspapers with their letters. Some of the letters were so venomous that the editorial page editor of the *Denver Post* admitted that her liberal faith had been shaken."[7] When CBS carried the story, a prominent evolutionist made the teenager out to be an enemy of education. Orthodoxy is not to be questioned.

One of the most significant factors in establishing the reign of evolution was the movie *Inherit the Wind,* the imaginative retelling of the story of the Scopes "Monkey Trial" of 1925. The trial is presented as a David-and-Goliath match between the few reasonable and enlightened advocates of progress and the forces of ignorance and oppression who are shackled by their "Old-Time Religion." The important players were caricatured and significant details were completely falsified, but the point was made: Religion can coexist with science, but only if it minds its own business.

The book *Defeating Darwinism* is an important contribution not only because of the questions it raises about evolution but also because it teaches the reader *how* to think about issues.

Baloney Detectors Wanted

In *Defeating Darwinism by Opening Minds,* Johnson analyzes the role *Inherit the Wind* played in our thinking about the relation of religion and science. This was the play—and later the movie—which retold the story of the Scopes "Monkey Trial." One significant character, who only appeared for a few minutes, was the Radio Man, the radio announcer who made a live broadcast from the courtroom.

Near the end of the play, when the prosecuting attorney launches into a long speech denouncing the evils of evolution, the radio program director decides that the attorney's speech has become boring, and Radio Man turns off the microphone. This is the only microphone in the courtroom. Johnson sees this move as symbolic. He says: "That is why what happened in the real-life Scopes trial hardly matters; the writers and producers of *Inherit the Wind* owned the microphone, making their interpretation far more important than the reality."[8]

This example illustrates one of several logical fallacies evolutionists sometimes commit which Johnson exposes in his chapter "Tuning Up Your Baloney Detector." This first fallacy is the selective use of evidence. Radio Man could broadcast what *he* wanted people to hear without giving the other side equal time. What we hear about today, says Johnson, are the evidences which *seem* to support evolution. What we *don't* hear about is the *absence* of significant evidence in the fossil record as a whole. Seeing the entire picture can, and should, easily give us doubts about the story we're now being told by the evolutionists.

Another fallacy evolutionists sometimes employ is the *ad hominem* argument, or the argument "against the man." If a doubter can be labeled a "fundamentalist" or a believer in "creation science" (meaning creation in six, twenty-four hour days), his doubts can be set aside on the grounds of religious prejudice.

Johnson cautions us to watch out also for "vague terms and shifting definitions." The word *evolution,* for example, can mean different things. Are we speaking of microevolution, small changes within a species, or are we talking about macroevolution, major mutations from one type of organism to another? As Johnson says, "That one word *evolution* can mean something so tiny it hardly matters, or so big it explains the whole history of the universe."[9]

Johnson notes that fewer than 10 percent of Americans actually believe that "humans . . . were created by a materialistic evolutionary process in which God played no part."[10] Nonetheless, the vast majority who doubt this are not allowed to think for themselves on the matter of evolution. Rather than being educated to think for themselves, students are indoctrinated with the dogmatic claims of evolutionists.

In response, Johnson urges students to discern whether what they are being taught is simply assumed or whether it is based on real evidence. When evolutionists insist on the *fact* of evolution without having concrete evidence, and without having any idea of the *mechanism* of evolution, they're revealing a faith commitment.

Intelligent Design

When Charles Darwin presented his theory of evolution, little was known about what goes on inside living cells. They were "black boxes," objects the insides of which were unknown. With the development of molecular biology, scientists have come to realize that cells are extremely complex.

In *Defeating Darwinism by Opening Minds,* Johnson introduces the reader to some exciting new discoveries in biology, which he believes deal a significant blow to Darwinian evolution.

Johnson says it's now recognized that there's information encoded in cells which can't be reduced to matter. Evolutionist Richard Dawkins writes, "Each nucleus . . . contains a digitally coded database larger, in information content, than all 30 volumes of the *Encyclopedia Britannica* put together. And this figure is for *each* cell, not all the cells of the body put together."[11]

This information is distinct from the physical structure in the same way that the message of a book is distinct from the ink and paper which records it. The question biologists must answer is, Where did this genetic information come from? Information implies intelligence. Physical mutations and natural selection can't explain it. This is a serious problem for Darwinists.

Another finding which also is a major problem for Darwinists is what is called the irreducible complexity of living organisms. Johnson explains what this means: "Molecular mechanisms . . . are made up of many parts that interact in complex ways, and all the parts need to work together. Any single part has no useful function unless all the other parts are also present."[12] The eye, for example, requires the coordinated working of many different parts to do its work. Each of these parts, however, can accomplish nothing on its own. That being the case, why would the individual parts have been preserved through time by natural selection? If there *was* gradual development, there must have been some intelligence behind it to know what to retain and what to destroy.

These two factors, then—information content and ir-reducible complexity—are strong physical evidence for intelligent design. Information implies intelligence, and mutation and selection can't account for complexity. It requires design.

In spite of the evidence, however, Darwinists still insist that the origin of life can't lie in supernatural creation. As we noted earlier, the key issue for them is their prior commitment to a naturalistic philosophy. As geneticist Richard Lewontin said, "[W]e are forced by our *a priori* adherence to material causes to create an apparatus of investigation and a set of concepts that produce material explanations, no matter how counter-intuitive. . . . Moreover, that materialism is absolute, for we cannot allow a Divine Foot in the door."[13]

It's Phillip Johnson's project to expose this prior commitment and to convince evolutionists to acknowledge it. Now we'll turn to look at Johnson's overall project and see what lessons we can draw from it.

Evaluation

Johnson calls his basic strategy for addressing the issue of evolution, the "wedge." He wants to drive a wedge into the "log" of scientific materialism so as to separate the facts of scientific investigation from the naturalistic philosophy, which dominates science.

One of the criticisms of Johnson's work is that he wants to throw the baby out with the bathwater. Theistic evolutionists, for example, say that one needn't accept a materialistic theory of evolution to recognize the gradual development of life on our planet. Indeed, Johnson seems to be fighting two battles: the first against those who insist upon doing science in a thoroughgoing naturalistic framework; the second against macroevolution of any sort.

I noted earlier that Johnson argues against separating the so-called *fact* of evolution from the *mechanism* of evolution. He insists that before we can know *that* evolution happened, we need to know *how* it happened. This certainly isn't a universal logical principle. I don't need to know precisely how a camera and film produce pictures to know *that* they do. Nonetheless, Johnson is correct in pressing for conclusive fossil evidence for gradual change or for a plausible explanation for sudden macromutations.

Johnson's challenge to the scientific community boils down to this question: "What should we do if empirical evidence and materialist philosophy are going in different directions?"[14] In other words, Are you willing to abandon a theory of purposeless processes if the evidence weighs against such a theory? When scientists are willing to do this, then science will be free to discover—as far as it's able—what nature is really like apart from personal prejudices.

It's evident that Johnson has struck a nerve in the scientific community. He's debated well-known scientists and has spoken at prestigious universities across America and overseas. He has not allowed opponents to pin him down on a particular theory of creation and then to dismiss him with the usual "religion vs. science" argument.

Johnson notes that Marx, Freud, and Darwin were three of the most influential men in this century. Marxism and Freudianism have both passed into history. Says Johnson, "I am convinced that Darwin is next on the block. His fall will be by far the mightiest of the three."[15]

But this will only happen, he says, if we "step off the reservation" and do the work necessary to prove our case.[16] We must encourage our young people to take up the challenge of thinking for themselves on this matter and not be intimidated by those who wish to maintain the status quo. This will involve a risk. If we teach our young people to think critically about evolution, they will eventually turn their attention on their own faith. But this is precisely what our young people need to do to make their faith their own. Christianity can stand the scrutiny. And as Johnson says: "We will never know how great the opportunity was if we are afraid to take the risk."[17]

This book is valuable for any Christian who wants to learn how to think critically, whether the reader is scientifically minded or not. Here we find a model for turning the tables on those who want to keep us on the defensive. If we have to give an answer for what we believe, it's only fair that our critics should do the same. *Defeating Darwinism* is an example of how to get them to do it.

9

Darwin's Black Box

Ray Bohlin

What do mousetraps, molecular biology, blood clotting, Rube Goldberg machines, and irreducible complexity have in common? At first glance there seems to be little if anything. However, they are all part of a book by Free Press titled *Darwin's Black Box: The Biochemical Challenge to Evolution* by Michael Behe, a biophysics professor at Lehigh University in Pennsylvania. His book, published in 1996, has been causing a firestorm of activity in academic circles ever since its release.

The stranglehold that Darwinism has had in the biological sciences for decades has already been weakened over the last thirty years due to the new creationist movement and more recently by the push from intelligent-design theorists. But Behe's new book may end up being the straw that breaks the camel's back. Usually books like this are released by Christian publishers, or at least a secular press that is small and willing to take a chance. Also, creationist books are rarely sold in secular bookstores or reviewed in secular publications. *Darwin's Black Box* has gained the attention of evolutionists not normally accustomed to responding to antievolutionary ideas in the academic arena. People like Niles Eldredge from the American Museum of Natural History, Daniel Dennett, author of *Darwin's*

Dangerous Idea, Richard Dawkins of Oxford University and author of *The Blind Watchmaker,* Jerry Robison of Harvard University, and David Hull from the University of Chicago have all been forced to respond to Behe either in print or in person.

The reason for all this attention is that they readily admit Behe is a reputable scientist from a reputable institution, and his argument is, therefore, more sophisticated than they are accustomed to hearing from creationists. Backhanded compliments aside, they unreservedly say he is flat wrong, but they have gone to great lengths from the podium, in writing, and in the electronic media to explain precisely why they think so. The works of creationists and intelligent-design theorists are usually dismissed out of hand, but not Behe's *Darwin's Black Box.*

Behe's simple claim is that when Darwin wrote *On the Origin of Species,* the cell was a mysterious black box. We could see the outside of it, but we had no idea how it worked. In *The Origin* Darwin stated, "If it could be demonstrated that any complex organ existed, which could not possibly have been formed by numerous, successive, slight modifications, my theory would absolutely break down. But I can find no such case."[1]

Simply put, Behe has found such a case. Behe claims that through the last forty years of research in molecular and cell biology the black box of the cell has been opened. In the cell numerous examples of complex molecular machines have been found that invalidate the theory of natural selection as an explanation of living systems. The power and logic of Behe's examples prompted *Christianity Today* to name *Darwin's Black Box* their 1996 Book of the Year.[2] Quite a distinction for a book on science published by a secular publisher!

In this chapter I will examine a few of Behe's examples and detail further how the scientific community has been reacting to this highly readable and influential book.

Irreducible Complexity and Mousetraps

Behe claims that the data of biochemistry argues against the theory that the molecular machines in the cell arose through a step-by-step process of natural selection. On the contrary, Behe writes, much of the molecular machinery in the cell is irreducibly complex.

Let me first address this concept of irreducible complexity. It's really quite a simple concept. Something is irreducibly complex if it's composed of several parts, and each part is absolutely necessary for the structure to function. The implication is that such irreducibly complex structures or machines cannot be built by natural selection, because in natural selection each component must be useful to the organism as the molecular machine is built. Behe uses the example of a mousetrap. A mousetrap has five parts, each of which are absolutely necessary for the mousetrap to function. Take any one of these parts away and the mousetrap can no longer catch mice. It is not just less efficient, catching fewer mice; the mousetrap catches nothing at all! In the biological world this means that there is nothing for nature to select. There is no function.

The mousetrap must contain a solid base onto which all the other parts attach. It must contain a hammer that clamps down on the mouse, a spring which gives the hammer the necessary power, a bar which holds the now-energized hammer in position, and a catch by which the holding bar is secured, thus keeping the hammer in coiled tension. Eventually, the jiggling action of a mouse, lured to the catch by a tasty morsel of peanut butter, causes the holding bar to slip away from the catch, releasing the hammer. So much for the unsuspecting mouse!

It's fairly easy to imagine the complete breakdown of functionality if you take away any of these five parts. Without the base, the other parts can't maintain the proper stability and distance from each other; without the spring or hammer, there is no way to actually catch the mouse; and without both the catch and holding bar, there is no way to set the trap. All the parts must be present in order for the machine to function at all and for a mouse to be caught.

You can't build a mousetrap by Darwinian natural selection. Let's say you have a factory that produces all five parts of a mousetrap but uses them for different purposes. Over the years as the production lines change, leftover parts of no-longer-made contraptions are put aside on shelves in a storage room. One summer, the factory is overrun with mice. If someone were to put his mind to it, he might run by the storage room and begin to play around with these leftover parts. He just might construct a mousetrap. But those pieces, left to themselves, are never going to spontaneously self-assemble into a mousetrap. A hammerlike part may accidentally fall from its box into a box of springs, but it's useless until all five parts are assembled so they can function together.

We have learned, Michael Behe claims, that several of the molecular machines in the cell are just as irreducibly complex as a mousetrap and, therefore, cannot be constructed by natural selection. Nature would select against the continued production of the miscellaneous parts if those parts were not producing an immediate benefit to the organism.

The Mighty Cilium

One of Behe's examples is the cilium. Cilia are tiny hairlike structures on the outside of cells that either help move fluid over a stationary cell, such as those in your lungs, or serve to propel a cell through water, as in the single-celled paramecium. There are often many cilia on the surface of a cell, and you can watch them beat in unison the way a stadium crowd performs the wave at a ball game.

A cilium operates like paddles in a rowboat; however, since it is a hairlike structure, it can bend. There are two actions in the operation of a cilium: the power stroke and the recovery stroke. The power stroke starts with the cilium essentially parallel to the surface of the cell. While the cilium is held rigid, it lifts up, anchored at its base in the cell membrane, and pushes backward through the liquid until it has moved nearly 180 degrees from its previous position. In the recovery stroke, the cilium bends near the base, and the bend moves down the length of the cilium as it hugs the surface of the cell until it reaches its previous stretched out position, again having moved 180 degrees back to its original position. How does this microscopic hairlike structure do this? Studies have shown that three primary proteins are necessary, though over two hundred other proteins are utilized.

If you took a cross-section of a cilium and made a photograph of it with an electron microscope, you would see that the internal structure of the cilium is composed of a central pair of fibers surrounded by an additional nine pairs of these same fibers arranged in a circle. These fibers or microtubules are long hollow sticks made by stacking the protein tubulin. The bending action of cilia depends on the vertical shifts made by these microtubules.

The bending is caused by another protein, called *nexin,*

that is stretched between the pairs of tubules. Nexin acts as a sort of rubber band connector between the tubules. As the microtubules shift vertically, the rubber band is stretched taut, the microtubules continue to shift if they bend. I know this is getting complicated, but stay with me a little longer! The microtubules slide past each other by the action of a motor protein called *dynein*. The dynein protein also connects two microtubules together. One end of the dynein remains stationary on one microtubule, while the other end releases its hold on the neighboring microtubule and reattaches a little higher, pulling the other microtubule down.

Without the motor protein, the microtubules don't slide and the cilium simply stands rigid. Without *nexin,* the tubules will slide against each other until they completely move past each other and the cilium disintegrates. Without the tubulin, there are no microtubules and no motion. The cilium is irreducibly complex. Like the mousetrap, it has all the properties of design and none of the properties of natural selection.

Rube Goldberg Blood Clotting

Rube Goldberg was a cartoonist in the earlier part of the twentieth century. He became famous for drawing weird contraptions—contraptions that had many unnecessary steps in order to accomplish a rather simple purpose. Over the years, some evolutionists have alluded to living systems as Rube Goldberg machines. They say the unnecessarily complicated mechanisms of these systems prove they evolved by natural selection as opposed to being designed by a Creator. For them, things such as the Panda's thumb and the intricate workings of the many varieties of orchid are contrived structures that an intelligent Creator would surely have found a better way of putting together.

If you have never seen a cartoon of a Rube Goldberg machine, let me describe one for you from Mike Behe's book, *Darwin's Black Box.* This one is titled the "Mosquito Bite Scratcher." Water falling off a roof flows into a drain pipe and collects in a flask. In the flask a cork floats up as the glass fills. Inserted in the cork is a needle that eventually rises high enough to puncture a suspended paper cup filled with beer. The beer then sprinkles onto a nearby bird that becomes intoxicated and falls off its platform onto a spring. The spring propels the inebriated bird onto another platform where the bird pulls a string (no doubt mistaking it for a worm in its intoxicated state). The pulled string fires a cannon underneath a small dog, frightening him and causing him to flip over on his back. His rapid breathing raises and lowers a disk above his stomach, which is attached to a needle positioned next to a mosquito bite on a man's neck allowing the bite to be scratched, causing no embarrassment to the man while he talks to a lady.

This machine is obviously more complicated than it needs to be. But the machine is still designed and as Behe claims, it is also irreducibly complex. In other words, if one of the steps fails or is absent, the machine doesn't work. The whole contraption is useless. Well, there are a few molecular mechanisms in our bodies that are very similar to Rube Goldberg machines. One is the blood-clotting cascade. When you cut your finger an amazing thing happens. Initially, it begins to bleed, but if you just leave it alone, after a few minutes, the flow of blood stops. A clot has formed, providing a protein mesh that initially catches the blood cells and eventually closes up the wound entirely, preventing the plasma from escaping as well.

This seemingly straightforward process involves over a dozen different proteins with names like thrombin, fibrinogen, Christmas, Stuart, and accelerin. Some of these proteins are involved in forming the clot. Others are responsible for regulating clot formation. Regulating proteins are needed because you only want clots forming at the site of a wound not in the middle of flowing arteries. Yet other proteins have the job of removing the clot once it is no longer needed. The body needs to eliminate the clot when it has outlived its usefulness, but not before.

It's easy to see why some, when considering the blood-clotting cascade, wonder if a Creator wouldn't have devised something simpler. But that assumes we fully understand the system. Perhaps it needs to be this way. Besides, this doesn't in any way diminish the fact that even a Rube Goldberg machine is designed, just as the blood-clotting system seems to be.

Silence of Molecular Evolution and the Reaction

Clearly, the irreducible complexity inherent in many biochemical systems not only precludes the possibility that they evolved by Darwinian natural selection but actually promotes the conclusion that some kind of intelligent design is necessary.

Behe makes a significant point by recognizing that, though the data implies intelligent design, it doesn't necessarily mean one knows who the designer is. Inferring the presence of intelligent design is a reasonable scientific conclusion. Planetary astronomers, for example, claim that we will be able to distinguish a radio signal sent by an intelligent civilization in space from the surrounding radio noise, even though we won't initially understand what it says and won't know who sent it.

Yet the astounding complexity of the cell has hardly been noted and reported to the general public. There is an embarrassed silence. Behe speculates about the reason. He says, "Why does the scientific community not greedily embrace its startling discovery? Why is the observation of design handled with intellectual gloves? The dilemma is that while one side of the elephant is labeled intelligent design, the other side might be labeled God."[3]

This may also help to account for another curious omission that Behe highlights—the relative absence of scientific literature attempting to describe how complex molecular systems could have arisen by Darwinian natural selection. The *Journal of Molecular Evolution* was established in 1971, dedicated to explaining how life at the molecular level came about. One would hope to find studies exploring the origin of complex biochemical systems in this journal. But, in fact, none of the papers published in *JME* has ever proposed the origin of a single complex biochemical system in a gradual step-by-step Darwinian process.

Furthermore, Behe adds, "The search can be extended, but the results are the same. There has never been a meeting, or a book, or a paper on details of the evolution of complex biochemical systems."[4]

Behe's sophisticated argument has garnered the attention of many within the scientific community. His book has been reviewed in the pages of *Nature, Boston Review, Wall Street Journal,* and on many sites on the Internet. While some have engaged in a genuine discussion of the ideas and offered serious rebuttal, most have sat back on Darwinian authority and claimed that Behe is just lazy or hasn't given the evolutionary establishment enough time. Jerry Coyne in *Nature* put it this way:

There is no doubt that the pathways described by Behe are dauntingly complex,
and their evolution will be hard to unravel.
Unlike anatomical structures, the evolution
of which can be traced with fossils, biochemical evolution must be reconstructed
from highly evolved living organisms, and
we may forever be unable to envisage the
first protopathways. It is not valid, however, to assume that, because one man cannot
imagine such pathways, they could not have
existed.[5]

But that's precisely the point; it is not one man but
the entire biochemical community that has failed to elu-
cidate a specific pathway leading to a complex biochemical
system.

I highly recommend Behe's book. Its impact will be
felt for many years to come.

Part 3
Evolution and Society

10

Sociobiology
Evolution, Genes, and Morality
Ray Bohlin

I n 1981 I wrote an article for *Christianity Today,* which they titled "Sociobiology: Cloned from the Gene Cult."[1] At the time I was fresh from a graduate program in population genetics and had participated in two graduate seminars on the subject of sociobiology. You might be thinking, "What in the world is sociobiology, and why should I care?"

Those are actually good questions. Sociobiology explores the biological basis of all social behaviors, including morality. Sociobiology maintains that not only have our physical bodies evolved by natural processes, but also our behaviors and societal structures. You should care, because sociobiologists are claiming that all moral and religious systems, including Christianity, exist simply because they help promote the survival and reproduction of the group. These sociobiologists, otherwise known as, evolutionary ethicists and evolutionary psychologists claim to be able to explain the existence of every major world religion or belief system, including Christianity, Judaism, Islam, and even Marxism and secular humanism, in terms of natural selection and evolution. In his recent book *Consilience,* E. O. Wilson, a Harvard biologist and major advocate of sociobiology, summarized: "Consider the alternative empiricist hypothesis, that precepts and religious faith are entirely material products of the mind. For more than a thousand generations they have increased the survival and reproductive success of those who conformed to tribal faiths. There was more than enough time for epigenetic rules—hereditary biases of mental development—to evolve that generate moral and religious sentiments. Indoctrinability became an instinct."[2]

Wilson claims that scientific materialism (a fully evolutionary worldview) will eventually overcome both traditional religion and any other secular ideology. While Wilson does admit that religion in some form will always exist, he suggests that theology, as an explanatory discipline, will soon become extinct. (He says this despite his claim that he was born again as a young teen. He rejected his faith in college when faced with the realities of evolution.)[3]

The First Paradox

While the arrogance of sociobiology is readily apparent, it contains a number of paradoxes. The first paradox is simply that its worldview offers nothing but despair when taken to its logical conclusion, yet it continues to gain acceptance in the academic community.

Four Foundational Principles of Sociobiology

The despair of the sociobiological worldview and the ultimate lack of meaning it presents are derived from what I consider the four foundational principles of sociobiology. *The first principle is the assertion that human social systems have been shaped by evolutionary processes.* This means that human societies exist in their present form because they work, or at least have worked in the past—not because they are based on any kind of truth or revelation.

Second, there is what sociobiologist Robert Wallace called the reproductive imperative.[4] The ultimate goal of any organism is to survive and reproduce. Species survival is the ultimate goal. Moral systems exist only because ultimately they promote human survival and reproduction.

Third, the individual, at least in respect to evolutionary time, is meaningless. Species, not individuals, evolve and persist through time. Therefore, the significance of the individual is swamped by the expanse of evolutionary time. But there is an even greater loss of dignity from a reductionist standpoint. You may have heard the old saying in biology that a chicken is just an egg's way of making another egg. Wilson has modernized this to say that your body is simply DNA's way of making more DNA.[5] The drive to reproduce is supposedly energized by the propensity of DNA, the hereditary material, to make copies of itself. Consequently, the organism is simply a vehicle for DNA to copy itself from generation to generation.

Fourth, all behaviors are therefore selfish, or at least pragmatic, at their most basic level. We love our children because love is an effective means of raising effective reproducers. Wilson spells out the combined result of these principles quite clearly in his book *On Human Nature* when he says that "no species, ours included, possesses a purpose beyond the imperatives created by its own genetic history (i.e., evolution) . . . we have no particular place to go. The species lacks any goal external to its own biological nature."[6]

Wilson is saying that since humans have been shaped by evolution alone, they have no purpose beyond survival and reproduction. Even Wilson admits that this is an unappealing proposition.

Hope and Meaning

When sociobiologists claim that all behavior is ultimately selfish, that an organism's only purpose is to survive and reproduce, and that it is species survival, not individual survival, that is ultimately required, personal worth and dignity quickly disappear. The responses of sociobiologists, if they are confronted with this conclusion, have always seemed curious to me. I distinctly remember posing a question about hope and purpose to a graduate seminar comprising biology students and faculty. I asked, "Let's suppose that I am dead and in the ground, and the decomposers are doing their thing. What difference does it make to me now whether I have reproduced or not?" My point was that if death is the end with a capital "E," who cares whether or not I have reproduced? After an awkward silence, one of the faculty answered, "Well, I guess that it doesn't matter at all."

In response, I asked, "Don't you see, we were just discussing how the only purpose in life is to survive and reproduce, but now you admit that this purpose is really an illusion. Why will people want to go on living if this is the case? Why stop at red lights? Who cares?" After an even longer silence, the same faculty member said, "Well, I suppose that those who will be selected in the future will be those who know there is no purpose in life, but will live as if there is."

To say the least, I was stunned by the frankness of his response. He was basically saying that the human race will be forced to live with a lie, the illusion of hope and meaning. What was even more unsettling, however, was the fact that no one disagreed or offered even the most remote protest. Apart from myself, everyone there accepted evolution as a fact, so they were forced to accept this conclusion.

(I found out later that at least a couple of them didn't like it, though they couldn't argue with its validity.)

A professor of philosophy at a university in Minnesota recently answered my challenge by saying that "maybe there are two different kinds of hope and meaning: hope and meaning in small letters (meaning survival and reproduction) and Hope and Meaning in capital letters (meaning ultimate worth and significance). We all have hope and meaning in small letters, and maybe there just aren't any in capital letters. So what?" But that was precisely my point; hope and meaning in small letters are without significance unless Hope and Meaning in capital letters really exist.

Three Responses

Over the years I have noted three responses of evolutionists to the stark reality that their worldview offers no hope or meaning in their lives. *The first is strong disagreement with the conclusions of sociobiology without strong reasons to justify their disagreement.* They don't like the result, but they find it difficult to argue with the basic principles. As evolutionists, they agree with evolution, but they don't want to believe that a meaningless existence is the end result. These individuals are left hoping there will be a way out some day. Meanwhile, they ignore the problem in their daily lives.

The second response is simple acceptance. These evolutionists agree that there is no purpose or meaning in life. They just have to accept it, as the professor in the story did. Their commitment to an evolutionary worldview is total. I find this attitude most prevalent among faculty and graduate students at secular institutions. There is an almost eerie fatalism. They stoutly embrace the notion that their dislike of a theory is not sufficient cause to raise questions about it, especially when it is based on "sound" evolutionary principles. Scientists holding this view will often present themselves as brave in the face of reality as opposed to those who choose to believe in the fairy tale of an afterlife. Never mind that their choice holds no meaning!

The third response is an existential leap for meaning and significance when both have been stripped away. Evolutionist Robert Wallace at the end of his book, *The Genesis Factor,* aptly illustrates this leap. For 217 pages Wallace tells us of the genetics of morality, the myth of altruism, the reproductive imperative—that genes are the devil that made you do it. Then suddenly out of nowhere, he writes:

> I do not believe that man is simply a clever egotist, genetically driven to look after his own reproduction. He is that. But he is at least that. He is obviously much more. The evidence for this is simple and abundant. One need only hear the "Canon in D Major" by Johann Pachelbel to know that there are immeasurable depths to the human spirit. But why am I telling you this? If you have ever stood alone in a dark forest and felt something akin to love, something utterly joyful, surge through you by simply putting your hand on the damp bark of a tree, then you know that the evolutionary explanation is not enough. What could have possessed Thoreau to walk two hours through the snow to spend the afternoon with a tree that

he knew? *A tree!* I am sorry for the person who has never broken into a silly dance of sheer exuberance under a starry sky: perhaps such a person will be more likely to interpret the message of this book more narrowly. The ones who will find it difficult to accept the narrow view are those who know more about the joy of being us. *My biological training is at odds with something that I know and something that science will not be able to probe,* perhaps because the time is now too short, perhaps because it is not measurable. I think our demise, if it occurs, will be a loss, a great loss, a great shame in some unknown equation.[7] (emphasis added)

What Wallace is saying in this passage is that something is missing, and it can't be found within the confines of the evolutionary worldview. So look wherever you can!

Some may argue that those who have trouble with the loss of hope and meaning are taking all this too seriously. I don't agree. On the contrary, I believe they are being consistent within their worldview. If everything has evolved, and there is nothing outside of mere biology to give meaning and significance to life, then we must live in despair, denial, or irrational hope.

Sociobiology is gaining in popularity because of the scientific community's strong commitment to evolution. If something follows logically from evolutionary theory, which I believe sociobiology does, then eventually all who consider themselves evolutionists will embrace it, whether it makes them comfortable or not. They will have no other rational choice.

The Second Paradox

In reflecting on the notion that all human societies and moral systems should have characteristics that seem to have evolved, I am led to a second paradox for sociobiology. The first paradox was that, despite the loss of hope and meaning in the context of a completely naturalistic worldview, sociobiology has continued to grow in influence. The second paradox involves Christianity. Since Christianity is based on revelation, it should be antithetical to or unexplainable by sociobiology, at least in some crucial areas.

It is not unreasonable to expect that some aspects of Christian morality would be consistent with a sociobiological perspective. Since Christians in small and large groups do work for the betterment of the group as a whole, the argument could be made that the survival of individuals is thus increased. However, if Christianity's claim that it is based on revelation from a transcendent God is true, I would be surprised, indeed extremely disappointed and confused, if everything in Christianity's moral standards also made sense from a sociobiological perspective. What little I have seen in the way of an evaluation of Christianity from E. O. Wilson and other sociobiologists is a poor caricature of true Christianity.

I would like to offer a few suggestions for consideration. William Irons, in a discussion of the evolution of moral systems, comments that nepotism is a very basic element of evolutionary theory.[8] Humans would have to be less competitive with and more helpful toward relatives than toward nonrelatives. He cites numerous studies to back up his claim that this prediction, more than any other sociobiological prediction, has been extensively confirmed.

To be sure, the New Testament considers the family very important. Church leaders are to be judged first by how they conduct themselves with their families (1 Tim. 3:12; Titus 1:6). Yet Jesus makes it quite clear that if there is any conflict between devotion to Him and devotion to family, family comes second. He said,

> Do not think that I came to bring peace on the earth; I did not come to bring peace, but a sword. For I came to set a man against his father, and a daughter against her mother, and a daughter-in-law against her mother-in-law; and a man's enemies will be the members of his household. He who loves father or mother more than Me is not worthy of Me; and he who loves son or daughter more than Me is not worthy of Me. And he who does not take his cross and follow after Me is not worthy of Me. He who has found his life shall lose it, and he who has lost his life for My sake shall find it. (Matt.10:34–39 NASB)

In other passages Jesus promises that if we give up our families and possessions for His sake, then we will receive abundantly more in this life and the next, along with the persecutions (Mark 10:29–30). Jesus Himself preferred the company of those who did the will of God to His own mother and brothers (Matt. 12:46–50). The clear message is that, while our families are important, our relationship with the living God comes first, even if members of our family force us to choose between God and them. Sociobiology may respond by saying that perhaps the benefit to be gained by inclusion in the group will compensate for the family loss, but how can the loss of an individual's entire genetic contribution to the next generation be explained away by any evolutionary mechanism?

Common Ground

So far I have concentrated my remarks in areas where a Christian worldview is in sharp contrast with the evolutionary worldview of the sociobiologists. Now I would like to explore an area of curious similarity.

While Christianity should not be completely explainable by sociobiology, there are certain aspects of Christian truth that are quite compatible with it. I have always been amazed by the curious similarity between the biblical description of the natural man or the desires of the flesh and the nature of man according to evolutionary principles. Both perceive people as selfish creatures at heart, looking out for their own interests. It is not "natural" for people to be concerned with the welfare of others unless there is something in it for them.

Sociobiology seems to be quite capable of predicting many of the characteristics of human behavior. Scripture, on the other hand, informs us that the natural man does not accept the things of the Spirit, that they are foolishness to him (1 Cor. 2:14). I have wondered if our sin nature is somehow enveloped by biology, or, to be more specific, genetics. Could it be that some genetic connection to our sin nature at least partially explains why there is no one righteous, there is no one who understands, there is no one who seeks for God (Rom. 3:10–11)? Does a genetic transmission of a sin nature help explain why all have sinned and fallen short of the glory of God (Rom. 3:23)? Is this why salvation can only be through faith—that it is not of ourselves, not a result of works, but a gift of God (Eph. 2:8–9)? Is this why the flesh continues to war in our bodies so that we do the thing we do not want to do, why nothing good dwells in us, and why the members of our bodies wage war against the laws of our minds (Rom. 7:14–25)?

If there is a genetic component to our sin nature, it seems reasonable to assume that only the Spirit of God can overcome the desires of the flesh. Clearly then, this struggle will continue in the believer until he or she is changed—until we see God face to face (1 Cor. 13:12; 15:50–58).

I ask these questions not thinking that I have come upon some great truth or the answer to a long-standing mystery, but simply looking for some common ground between the truth of Scripture and the truth about human nature from the perspective of sociobiology. All truth is ultimately God's truth. While I certainly do not embrace the worldview of the sociobiologist, I realize that there may be some truth that can be discovered by sociobiologists and truly captured to the obedience of Christ (2 Cor. 10:5).

When I wrote that article for *Christianity Today* in 1981, I closed with this paragraph: "To know what to support and what to oppose, Christians involved in the social and biological sciences must be effective students of sociobiology. The popularity of sociobiology has gone unnoticed for too long already. We need precise and careful study as well as a watchful eye if we are to take every thought captive to the obedience of Christ."[9]

11

Evolution and the Pope

Rich Milne

We have just passed the one hundredth anniversary of one of the most important books written about the interaction of science and Christianity. The book's title, *A History of the Warfare of Science with Theology in Christendom,*[1] says much about the book. Andrew White wrote it in 1896 to justify his belief that a university should be without any religious affiliation. He was the founder and first president of Cornell University in New York and was outspoken in his views about the hindrance religion has been to scientific progress. It was White who popularized the idea that there was a war between science and Christianity and that, in all cases, science had ultimately been proven to be right.

A History of the Warfare of Science with Theology in Christendom is one long polemic attempting to show that religion has always held back the advance of science. The author maintains that if theology would quit sticking its nose into the tent of science, everyone would be better off. The book was regarded, well into this century, as an important statement on the tension between science and religion. One hundred years, however, has changed the tone of the discussion. For several reasons, it has come to be commonly accepted that Christianity has played a key role in preparing the way for the development of modern science.[2]

First, Christians assumed they lived in a world that could be understood because it was created by a rational God—the same God who had also created them. This gave early scientists some reason to assume that nature might obey laws that could be known.

Second, not only was the universe understandable because a rational God made it but the Bible encouraged believers to look at God's creation for signs of His handiwork. For example, as early as the Psalms David had proclaimed, "The heavens are telling of the glory of God" (Ps. 19:1 NASB). Scripture passages such as this one, and many others, encouraged Christians to study nature to understand how it glorified God. Christians were confident that nature's design would show forth God's glory.

However, in the nineteenth and twentieth centuries much happened to erode Christians' confidence that they lived in a world crafted by God. In particular, Darwin's theory (that all organisms were descended from a common ancestor and that any appearances of design could be explained by natural selection working over long periods of time) came to have great acceptance among almost all scientists. For many the theory of evolution was seen as the reason why the world is as it is. For them, there was no need at all for a Creator or God to explain anything, because evolution could, or would, explain everything. British evolutionist Richard Dawkins has said, "Atheism might have been *logically* tenable before Darwin. Darwin made it possible to be an intellectually fulfilled atheist."[3]

A notable example of this position is the famous statement by astronomer Carl Sagan, "The universe is all that is or ever was or ever will be."[4] With these words he began

his immensely popular series about the universe, *Cosmos.*
His words are the creed of the materialist—that is, if it
can be counted, measured, observed, experimented on,
understood by natural laws, then it is real; anything else
is either meaningless or, at least, not scientific.

According to this view, mountain goats are real because we can see them, touch them, and put them in zoos.
Angels, on the other hand, are not real because we can do
none of these things to them. Science has to do with facts,
and if there is any place for religion it is in the consideration of morals or ethics or those other areas where there
are no facts.

But some people, such as Stephen Jay Gould, a paleontologist at Harvard, have remained open to the coexistence
of religion and science. In his monthly column for *Natural
History* magazine, he recently elaborated on how evolution,
science, and religion are connected.[5] His proposed resolution
of this issue is the theme of this chapter.

Gould proposes a complete answer to the problem of
how science and religion relate to one another. Simply put,
they don't interact at all. "The net of science," says Gould,
"covers the empirical universe: what it is made of (fact)
and why it works this way (theory). The net of religion
extends over questions of moral meaning and value. These
two magisteria do not overlap."[6]

The Roman Catholic Church uses the term *magisterium*
to refer to the areas of its authority—areas relating to the
Bible and its interpretation. Gould borrows this term and
applies it to the area that science claims as its own. So the
church may speak about moral issues, and science about
matters of fact and theory. For this somewhat unbalanced
division, he creates the wonderful phrase "nonoverlapping
magisteria."

Has the Pope's View of Evolution Evolved?

Gould is certainly free to pontificate. However, what is somewhat mystifying is how he draws in Pope John Paul II as a prime supporter not only of his interesting distinction between science and religion but also of evolution!

On October 22, 1996, Pope John Paul II addressed the Pontifical Academy of Sciences. The theme of its conference was the origin of life and evolution, so John Paul helpfully laid out what the church had said over the last fifty years.

The pope made it clear that his predecessor, Pope Pius XI, had "considered the doctrine of 'evolutionism' a serious hypothesis." But, John Paul said, "Today, almost half a century after the publication of the encyclical [of Pius XI], new knowledge has led to the recognition of the theory of evolution as more than a hypothesis. It is indeed remarkable that this theory has been progressively accepted by researchers, following a series of discoveries in various fields of knowledge. The convergence, neither sought nor fabricated, of the results of work that was conducted independently is in itself a significant argument in favor of this theory."[7]

That is as far as John Paul's statement goes: Evolution has moved from a serious hypothesis to a theory with significant arguments in its favor.

Yet from this statement, Gould triumphantly draws an amazing observation: "In conclusion, Pius had grudgingly admitted evolution as a legitimate hypothesis that he regarded as only tentatively supported and potentially (as I suspect he hoped) untrue. John Paul, almost fifty years later . . . adds that additional data and theory have placed the factuality of evolution beyond reasonable doubt.

Sincere Christians must now accept evolution not merely as a plausible possibility, but also as an effectively proven fact."[8]

Is this really what the pope said?

Does Evolution Fit the Truth About Man?

Stephen Gould has the pope saying something significant. From Gould's point of view, he is conceding defeat. How does Gould paraphrase John Paul's statement? "Sincere Christians must now accept evolution not merely as a plausible possibility, but also as an effectively proven fact."

Nevertheless, either by reading too rapidly or possessing too much enthusiasm for his own position, Gould misses critical distinctions that the pope's announcement makes. To argue that the pope's statement ("new knowledge has led to the recognition of the theory of evolution as more than a hypothesis") means that "sincere Christians must now accept evolution not merely as a plausible possibility, but also as an effectively proven fact" is ludicrous. Gould almost twists the pope's statement to contradict what the pope actually *does* say.

In fact, in his next paragraph, the pope states: "A theory is a metascientific elaboration, distinct from the results of observation but consistent with them. . . . Furthermore, while the formulation of a theory like evolution complies with the need for consistency with observed data, it borrows certain notions from natural philosophy."[9]

Metascientific means "going beyond the realms of science into an abstract, philosophical arena." So the pope says evolution is more than a hypothesis; it is a theory. But as such, it also is "distinct from the results of observation" and borrows from philosophy. His next statement is one Gould may have skipped over: "And, to tell the truth, rather than the theory of evolution, we should speak of several theories of evolution. On the one hand, this plurality has to do with the different explanations advanced for the mechanism of evolution, and on the other, with the various philosophies on which it is based. Hence the existence of materialist, reductionist and spiritualist interpretations."[10]

So rather than saying the words Gould puts in his mouth, the pope actually says that not only is evolution based on a philosophy, but there are several theories. He goes on to rule out some of them, at least for Roman Catholics. "Theories of evolution which, in accordance with the philosophies inspiring them, consider the spirit as emerging from the forces of living matter or as a mere epiphenomenon of this matter, are incompatible with the truth about man."[11]

Gould wants the pope to say, "You talk about science, and I'll talk about religion. You can have the world of facts, and I'll take what's left. These areas won't overlap with each other, and we'll each stay in our own gardens." But the pope is unwilling to follow Gould's convenient (for science) scheme. Instead, he firmly declares "The Church's magisterium is directly concerned with the question of evolution, for it involves the conception of man."[12]

This is what all of us who are Christians should be saying. Evolution, as it is usually presented, is not just a theory about ancient data. It is also a philosophical statement about where humanity came from and what (if any) significance we humans have. While Gould claims his scientific views are not related to his moral views, his words give little support to this.

Is Christianity Concerned About Evolutionary Theories?

Early in his essay Gould dismisses creationists with a few quick paragraphs. "Creationism does not pit science against religion, for no such conflict exists. Creationism does not raise any unsettled intellectual issues about the nature of biology or the history of life. Creationism is a local and parochial movement, powerful only in the United States among Western nations, and prevalent only among the few sectors of American Protestantism that chooses to read the Bible as an inerrant document, literally true in every jot and tittle."[13] Well, so much for a fair, informed assessment of one's opponents.

First he defines out of existence what creationists see as a central argument by merely saying "no such conflict exists." Then he proceeds to caricature creationists as a fringe group only found among a small group of Protestants. Prior to this he has equated "scientific creationism," the view that the earth was created in six days and is "only a few thousand years old," with all of creationism, which includes those who believe in an earth billions of years old and an evolutionary process that God superintended.

Gould's claim that "creationism does not raise any unsettled issues" ignores significant questions about how life first arose from chemicals, about the source of the genetic code, and about the origination of new biological structures.

But does the pope truly believe in Gould's nonoverlapping magisteria? Gould begins his summation of John Paul's speech by summarizing Pius's older encyclical of 1950 and reaffirming the NOMA principle (nonoverlapping magisterial). Nothing new here.

But what did the pope really say? He begins by saying that "the origins of life and evolution [are] an essential subject which deeply interests the Church, since Revelation, for its part, contains teachings concerning the nature and origins. . . . I would like to remind you that the magisterium of the Church has already made pronouncements on these matters within the framework of her own competence."[14] This hardly sounds like there is no overlap between what the church teaches and science. Toward the end of his remarks, John Paul flatly contradicts Gould's neat distinction: "The Church's magisterium is directly concerned with the question of evolution for it involves the conception of man." So it would seem that Gould has used those parts of the pope's speech which he likes and disregarded the rest.

Two points are important here. First, while Gould presents an interesting view on the relationship between science and religion and gives a new name to what used to be called "complementarity," it is not the view espoused by the pope. It is almost antithetical to it.

Second, Gould himself does not abide by this strict separation in expressing his own views, even when he claims to. When Gould actually makes his own moral position clear, it is hard to escape the conclusion that it comes directly from his views and philosophy as a scientist.

Why Trust Your Mind If No One Made It?

Gould's position, which he immediately claims is not "a deduction from my knowledge of nature's factuality" is, "Nature was not constructed as our eventual abode, didn't know we were coming . . . and doesn't give a _____ about us (speaking metaphorically)." He says he finds such a view "liberating . . . because we then become free to conduct moral discourse . . . in our own terms, spared from the delusion that we might read moral truth passively from nature's factuality."[15] It is indeed hard *not* to draw the conclusion that Gould has read his view about the process of evolution into his own moral position. How does he know that nature was not constructed for us if not from his studies of the natural world? How would he know it doesn't care about us unless somehow he saw this in his studies? Where else might he get such ideas?

Gould has a materialist philosophy behind his theory of evolution. He believes that the material universe is all that exists, and that our own consciousness does not come from a Creator but is a chance phenomenon. So, for Gould, where else can he obtain his views about morality and the meaning of life? His very thinking is the chance product of an evolutionary process that had no design, either to produce human beings or to give them minds. Nonetheless, Gould trusts his mind not only to distinguish between science and religion but to decide that they should not influence one another.

Gould's view is a version of the common denominator of much of science today. At all costs religion must be kept out of science or else science will cease to exist. Only material answers can be given to any question because the intervention of a Creator would negate the laws that govern science. What is missed in all of this is that, without a Creator of some kind, not only is there no basis for trusting the human mind to make true observations but there is no reason to suppose that it would matter. Why worry about science or religion, and certainly why worry about whether they could have a negative effect on each other? If there is no God, there can only be arbitrary judgments. It is God who gives meaning to what we say and believe.

Christians serve a rational God who made both them and the world. On what does Gould base his trust in either science or the mind?

Part 4
Evolution and the Bible

12

How to Talk to Your Kids About Evolution and Creation

Ray and Sue Bohlin

My wife, Sue, and I will discuss in an interactive format how to talk to kids about creation and evolution. It's one thing to have technical information at your fingertips for discussions with other adults, but when your kids ask you about evolution, dinosaurs, and cavemen, you need different data. So, with Sue's help, I will distill some of the technical stuff and steer through some of the minefields of uncertainty that exist in this crucial area. Sue's questions and comments are in italic type and are followed by my answers.

Problems with Evolutionary Theory

Why is there a problem with evolution in the first place? Someone once asked you, "What should I believe?" Remember what you told them?

Basically I said you should only believe what there is evidence for. After spending years studying evolution in bachelor's, master's, and doctoral programs, I can tell you

that, first of all, there is evidence for small changes in organisms as they adapt to small environmental fluctuations.
Second, there is evidence that new species do arise. We
see new species of fruit flies, rodents, and even birds. But
when the original species is a fruit fly, the new species is
still a fruit fly. These processes do not tell us how we get
horses and wasps and woodpeckers and scientific observers.

Third, in the fossil record, there are only a few transitions
between major groups of organisms, as between reptiles
and birds, and these are controversial even among evolutionists. If evolutionary theory is correct, the fossil record
should be full of them.

Fourth, there are no real evolutionary answers for the
origin of complex adaptations like the tongue of the woodpecker; or flight in birds, mammals, insects, and reptiles;
or the swimming adaptations in fish, mammals, reptiles,
and the marine invertebrates. These adaptations appear in
the fossil record with no transitions.

And fifth, there is no genetic mechanism for these
large-scale evolutionary changes. The theory of evolution
from amoeba to man is an extrapolation from meager data.

So the problem with evolution is that it is a mechanistic
theory without a mechanism, and there is no evidence for
the big changes from amoeba to humanity.

*I have our son's eighth-grade biology textbook here. Every text-
book, including this one, has a story about the evolution of the
horse. It is always offered as proof of evolution. What do you say?*

It does not prove much about evolution at all. David
Raup, from the Field Museum of Natural History in
Chicago, says: "We are now about 120 years after Darwin,
and knowledge of the fossil record has been greatly ex-
panded. Ironically, we have even fewer examples of

evolutionary transition than we had in Darwin's time. By this I mean that some of the classic cases of Darwinian change in the fossil record, such as the evolution of the horse in North America, have had to be discarded or modified as a result of more detailed information."[1]

There is no simple chronological sequence of horse-like fossils. The story of the gradual reduction from the four-toed horse of 60 million years ago to the one-toed horse of today has been called pure fiction. All that can be shown is the transition from a little horse to a big one, with numerous side branches moving from North America to Europe and back again. This is not significant evolutionary change, and it still took some 60 million years. It says nothing about how the horse evolved from a shrewlike mammal.

Homologous and Vestigial Organs

Homologous organs: What are they?

Homologous organs are organs or structures in different organisms that have the same or similar function. Evolutionists say this similarity is due to common ancestry. The important question is, Do these organs look and function the same because of common ancestry or because of a simple common design. In other words, do they look this way because they are related to one another, or were they designed to perform a similar function, but are unrelated? Homology is not a problem for creationists; we have a different but reasonable explanation. It is the result of common design, not common ancestry.

Often when genetic background can be investigated, we find that the supposedly same genes do not code for homologous structures. If different genes code for essentially the same structure, it becomes pretty difficult to explain how they can be evolutionarily related. For instance, it has always been assumed that the feathers of birds have their origin in the scales of reptiles. If this were the case, we should find some level of homology between scales and feathers. A recent study showed just the opposite: "The molecular evidence questions the simple, direct relation of the specialized structures of birds to reptile scale. I [can] provide arguments to show that reptilian scales and feathers are related only by the fact that their origin is in epidermal tissue. Every feature from gene structure and organization, to development, morphogenesis and tissue organization is different."[2]

What about vestigial organs, the ones that are supposedly left over from the evolutionary past? I remember being taught that the coccyx, the tailbone, is left over from when we were monkeys. And the appendix—we needed it when we were evolving, but we do not need it now.

That's right. According to evolutionary theory, vestigial organs are unused leftovers from our evolutionary past. Since we do not use them, they have diminished; they have become vestiges of their past functions.

But we have discovered that these structures do have a function. The prime example is the one you mentioned, the tailbone. The coccyx serves as a point of attachment for several pelvic muscles. You would not be able to sit very well or comfortably without a tailbone.

The appendix was also long thought to be a vestigial organ, having absolutely no function within our bodies, but now we find it is involved in the immune system. It does have a function. It is true that you can live without it. However, as we learn more about the appendix, we realize that if it remains uninfected, it may be serving a very useful purpose.

So in other words, "vestigial organs" are not necessarily use-less; we just may not have discovered what their role is.

Yes, very often we have called these things "vestigial." We never bothered to investigate their function because of their reduced stature. Now we find that things like the coccyx and the appendix really do have a function. And if they have a function, then we cannot call them vestigial; they are not leftovers from our evolutionary past. One other point about vestigial organs is that the creationist's posi-tion can easily accommodate structures or organs that are diminishing because of disuse. This is, after all, a fallen universe and things are not as God intended them to be. In addition, while evolution will point to any number of vestigial leftovers, what is critical are new structures that are evolving. Evolutionists are curiously quiet about this necessary, but absent, component of evolutionary theory.

I am looking, in this textbook, at pictures of embryos that are very similar. The explanation given in the book is that they are similar because they have a common evolutionary ancestor. Obviously, this is being advanced as evidence of evolution. Is that what it is?

Definitely not. Embryological development does not follow the history of our evolutionary past. That idea was proven wrong fifty or sixty years ago. It is unfortunate that this error is still in the textbooks. Obviously, there are some similarities among species very early in embryo-logical development—for instance, among mammals, reptiles, amphibians, and birds. But what evolutionists don't tell you is that the earliest stages of embryonic devel-opment in these same organisms are radically different.

Michael Denton documents that after fertilization, amphibian, reptile, and mammalian embryos follow different pathways. Eventually they converge to become embryos of similar appearance and then diverge again to become very different as newborn organisms. Rather than starting with identical fertilized eggs and slowly diverging, the embryos start differently, converge in the middle and differentiate from there. This sequence resembles more of an hourglass than the evolutionary prediction of an inverted pyramid.

It has also been recently documented that the drawings found in most biology textbooks of the similar stages of vertebrate embryos are all based on Ernst Haeckel's deliberately fudged drawings from the nineteenth century. Haeckel intentionally distorted the early embryonic stages to resemble each other in order to present a better case for evolution. Haeckel's deception was exposed in the late nineteenth century, but textbook writers seem to be unaware of the problem and routinely publish these falsified drawings.[3]

The Early Atmosphere of the Earth

You know, I was pretty happy with how this particular textbook treated evolution. It does not even use the word evolution, *and it treats it strictly as a matter of theory, not fact. But you showed me another, newer high school textbook that is stridently proevolution. I am concerned about some things I see in this chapter on the origin of life. It is talking about the earth's early atmosphere, and this statement is in bold print (so the students know it is going to be on the test, don't you know!): "The earth's first atmosphere most likely contained water vapor, carbon monoxide and carbon dioxide, nitrogen, hydrogen sulfide, and hydrogen cyanide." Then in the very next section it talks about Stanley Miller's famous experiments in 1953. It says the atmosphere he was trying to recreate was made of ammonia, water, hydrogen, and methane.[4] What is going on here?*

This particular section is confusing at best and misleading at worst. Clearly they have described Miller's classic experiment, but researchers today agree that the atmosphere used for that simulation did not exist. Yet, Miller's experiment produced results. If you use the atmosphere that the textbook describes as the real one, the results are much less significant. The textbook gives the impression that chemical evolution is easy to simulate. This is far from the truth. One experimenter says: "More than thirty years of experimentation on the origin of life in the fields of chemical and molecular evolution have led to a better perception of the immensity of the problem of the origin of life on earth rather than to its solution. At present, all discussions on principles and theories in the field either end in stalemate or in a confession of ignorance."[5]

But you would definitely not get that impression from reading this section of the textbook.

Phylogenetic Trees

I have another question. I'm looking at a beautiful, tidy chart that shows how neatly different animals evolved from one common ancestor. This evolutionary tree has a crocodile-like animal at the bottom, and all these branches coming out from him, and we end up with turtles and snakes and reptiles and birds and mammals, all descended from this one animal. Are we talking science fantasy here? Is there a problem with this evolutionary tree?

Evolutionary trees, or phylogenetic trees, are regularly misrepresented in high-school textbooks. The nice solid lines give the impression that there is plenty of evidence, plenty of fossils to document these transitions—but the transitions are not there. If we were to look at this same type of diagram in a college textbook, all those connecting lines—the transitions—would be dotted lines, indicating that we do not have the evidence to prove that these organisms are related. The transition is an assumption. They assume these organisms are related to each other, but the evidence is lacking. Stephen Jay Gould, a paleontologist and evolutionist from Harvard, says, "The extreme rarity of transitional forms in the fossil record persists as the trade secret of paleontology. The evolutionary trees that adorn our textbooks have data only at the tips and nodes of their branches. The rest is inference, however reasonable: not the evidence of fossils."[6]

In other words, these charts make pretty pictures, but they are not pictures of reality.
That's correct.

Natural Selection and Speciation

In this same high school biology text, I am looking at the chapter on evolution called "How Change Occurs." The big heading for this section is "Evolution by Natural Selection." Natural selection always seems to be linked inseparably to evolution. What is it?

Natural selection is a process by which the organisms that are fit to survive and reproduce do so at a greater rate than those that are less fit. It sounds circular, but it is a simple process, something you can easily observe in nature.

There are some pictures in this biology text of England's famous peppered moths. Why do they keep showing up in science textbooks?

They keep showing up because the peppered moth was the first documented example of Darwin's natural selection at work. There were two different colored varieties of the same moth: a peppered variety and a dark black variety. The peppered variety was camouflaged on the bark of trees by the lichens that grew there, but the black variety was conspicuous. As a result, the birds ate a lot of black moths. The most common variety, therefore, was the peppered variety. But then the lichens began to disappear and bark of the trees turned dark or black because of pollution. Now the dark form was hidden, but the peppered variety stood out, so the birds ate up the peppered variety. The proportion of peppered moths to black moths shifted in response to the change in the environment. At least this was the official story.

So here was a change of frequency. At one time we had more peppered moths, and now we have more dark ones—a clear example of natural selection taking place. But the question is, Is this really evolution? I don't think so. It just shows variety within a form. This does not tell me anything as a biologist and a geneticist about how we have come to have horses and wasps and woodpeckers.

In addition, the entire story of the peppered moth has been thrown into confusion. New studies indicate that the moths never rest on the trunks of trees. In some areas of Britain, the dark form took over even when there was no pollution-caused reduction of lichens on the trees. And actually, no one has ever seen a bird picking off a moth while it rested naturally in the upper reaches of a tree.[7]

When we are looking at peppered moths, we are dealing with natural selection within the same species. What about a whole new species, such as Darwin's Galapagos finches off the coast of Ecuador. Isn't that an evidence of evolution?

Here is another area where we need to be careful. Speciation is indeed a real process, but speciation only means that two populations of a particular species can no longer interbreed. A geographical barrier such as a mountain range separates the two populations, and after a time they are no longer able to interbreed or to reproduce between themselves.

But all we have really done is split up the gene pool into two different, separate populations; if you want to call them different species, that's fine. But even Darwin's finches, although there are some changes in the shape and size of the bill, are clearly related to one another. And new evidence demonstrates that several of the Galapagos finches can still interbreed and form viable hybrids.[8] Drosophila fruit flies on the Hawaiian Islands—there are more than three hundred species—probably originated from one initial species. They look very much the same. The primary way to distinguish them is by their mating behavior.

A lot of variety occurs within the organisms God created, and species can adapt to small changes in the environment. But there is a limit to how far that change can go. And the examples we have, like peppered moths and Darwin's finches, show that clearly.

Responding to Evolutionary Theory

You have given a creationist's response to evolution in text-books, but apart from the books there is a personal issue to deal with. How do you think Christian students should react when they face evolution in a science curriculum in school?

First, don't panic. This should not be a surprise—you knew it was going to come eventually.

Second, understand that evolution is a very important idea in society today. It is good to know about it and to understand it. Try to explain it to your kids in that way. You do not have to believe it or accept it, but you need to understand it, and know what people mean when they talk about evolution.

What about answering a question on a test?

Here it can get a little sticky. You may feel that you have to lie in order to give the answer the teacher wants. But I do not think that is the case at all. What you are doing is simply addressing the issue of evolution; you are showing that you understand it. You do not have to phrase your answer in such a way that says, "I believe this is the way it is." It may come down to how you state your answer. But you are simply demonstrating your knowledge about evolution, not your acceptance of it.

It seems to me that when you show you understand the concept of evolution, you are demonstrating respect for the teacher and for the prevalent theory of our day without having to make a statement of, "Yes, I believe this!"

Sure. The concept of respect, I think, is extremely important, because you have to realize that as a middle school or high school student, you are dealing with teachers who have studied or taught evolutionary theory for many years. Their level of understanding is much deeper than yours. You cannot simply go in there and try to convince the class that the teacher is wrong or that evolution is wrong. You need to play the role of a student, and the role of a student is to learn, to try to understand and comprehend the ideas being discussed. But you do not have to communicate in such a way that you appear to believe evolutionary theory.

Immediately following the chapter on evolution is this message from the authors to the students:

Evolutionary theory unites all living things into one enormous family—from the tallest redwoods to the tiniest bacteria to each and every human on Earth. And, most importantly, the evolutionary history of life makes it clear that all living things—all of us—share a common destiny on this planet. If you remember nothing else from this course ten years from now, remember this, and your year will have been well spent.[9]

I have never seen a message like this before, from the authors to the student. This textbook obviously has a strong evolution bias.

Here we have to realize that what is being taught is not science anymore; this is a worldview. This is a statement of naturalism. Obviously, evolution is extremely important to the naturalistic worldview, and the authors are trying to communicate its significance. We are going to see more and more of this bias in textbooks.

Before Christian parents can talk to their kids about evolution, we first must have an understanding of evolution itself and its problems. We do not need to be afraid of this powerful theory; we do, however, need discernment in sifting through the rhetoric and distinguishing it from the truth about God's world.

Genesis 1

Typically, if children spend any time at all in Sunday school, they gain the realization, Hey, this doesn't relate at all to what I'm learning in school! Our hope is that we can help parents integrate the truth of Scripture with what is known about origins in the world. As Christians, our starting point for thinking about origins is Genesis 1: "In the beginning God created the heavens and the earth." From that point on, though, there are a lot of different perspectives explaining the rest of the chapter.

That is true, and unfortunately it not only gets confusing for many of us, but it gets confusing for many of the academics and the scholars as well. There are a number of different ways to interpret Genesis 1. Let me just run through three of the most prominent views among evangelicals today.

The first is the *literal* or the *very recent* creation account. Some people would call the proponents of this view "young-earth creationists." They believe that each of the six days of creation was a twenty-four-hour period similar to our days today. These days were consecutive and in the recent past, probably ten to thirty thousand years ago. They hold that the Flood was a worldwide and catastrophic event and that most of the sedimentary layers and fossils were a result of it.

The second way of looking at Genesis 1 is the *day age theory,* sometimes called *progressive creation.* Here, each of the six days of creation is a very long period of time, perhaps hundreds of millions of years. God would have created progressively through time, not all at once. The Flood is a local event in Mesopotamia or perhaps even a worldwide, but tranquil, flood. Therefore, the Flood did not leave any great scars or sediments across the earth.

The third view understands Genesis 1 as a *literary framework.* This view suggests that Genesis 1 was not meant to communicate history. Peoples of the Ancient Near East used a similar literary device to describe a complete or perfect work—in this case, a perfect creation. God could have created using evolution or progressive creation; the point is that there is really no concordance between earth history and the days of Genesis 1.

We need to explain to our children the view that makes the most sense to us. But at the same time let them know that there is some disagreement between evangelicals. You may even be confused yourself, and it is okay to communicate to your children that you do not know either, and that not knowing is all right. We need to give direction but leave the doors open for various options. Genesis 1 leaves a lot of details out of the creation story. It is a brief account of the origin of everything, so it is reasonable that we would find areas of disagreement based on so little information.

Can we know which one is the correct interpretation?

Creation is a mystery. We need to show respect, not only for the mystery, but also for those people holding different views. Evangelicals with backgrounds in Hebrew and Greek differ on their understanding of Genesis 1. So how can we expect to grasp the problem and make an actual decision, let alone expect it of a ten-year-old?

When we explain the creation account in Genesis 1, we need to communicate to our children that different scholars, all committed to the Bible as the inerrant Word of God, interpret Scripture differently. The important thing is that we stress God's creation of the earth, the universe, and every living thing, especially humans. The actual process and timing are still left in some doubt.

Early Human History

Now we are going to look at some specific issues that arise from Genesis in terms of early human history. Let's start with Adam and Eve. Were they real people?

This is an important question, and I think it is one that most evangelical scholars can agree on. Adam and

Eve were real people, and almost all evangelical scholars agree that they were created by God. The reason is that this is the one creation event where God gives us details as to how He went about it. When He created the other mammals and the sea creatures and the birds, He "made" them or He "created" them or He "formed" them. We are given far more details about the creation of Adam and Eve. We are told how God did it. Adam was formed from dust, and Eve was created from Adam's side. It is clear that humans do not have an evolutionary origin.

What about australopithecines, those supposed apelike human ancestors?

Australopithecines most likely are extinct apes. Some quibble as to whether they walked upright and therefore may have been on their way to developing into human beings. But even if they did walk upright, that is not a real problem. They are still extinct apes, and they really had no human qualities whatsoever.

A very good book that you may want to look at is called *Bones of Contention.*[10] There are a couple of books called *Bones of Contention,* but this is a recent one by Marvin Lubenow. Lubenow goes into great detail about the actual fossil finds—what they mean, where they fit—all from a creationist's perspective, and he does a very good job. He talks about the fact that human remains seem to span the whole era of supposed human evolution from 4 million years ago to the present, and that even the one particular type of fossil called *Homo erectus* covers a broad range. *Homo erectus* does not really fit where he is supposed to, and the fossils seem to contradict evolutionary theory rather than support it.

One more question keeps coming up again and again. Where did Cain's wife come from?

In some ways it is surprising that this question seems to be so perplexing to people, but in another way I understand it. Clearly, Cain married a sister. We react against that idea because of the laws we have today concerning incestuous relationships. We have laws against incest because the children that result from that type of relationship are often afflicted with a genetic disease. This is because all of us carry detrimental recessive genes within our chromosomes. Closely related family members carry many of the same recessive genes. When we marry within the family, those recessives can pair up and result in a child who is handicapped. But in the original creation, there was no such problem. Adam and Eve were the first human beings, so there were no genetic mutations to worry about. Civilization had not had sufficient time for genetic mutations to accumulate in the population.

When it comes to human origins, the Bible gives no room for anything other than God's personal fashioning of Adam and Eve. It is the fact that God personally created humankind that gives us such intrinsic value.

Noah's Flood

Noah's flood is extremely important—but all too often what comes to mind when we think of it is the image of a cute little round boat with the heads of fluffy sheep, tall giraffes, and friendly elephants sticking out of it. We think of it as a harmless bedtime story like "Cinderella" or "Scuffy the Tugboat," a remnant of childhood Bible lessons and storybook times. Did the flood of Noah really happen?

We are talking about a historical event and one that was very serious. It is spoken of in Genesis in a historical narrative. But evangelicals do disagree about how it happened. There are basically three different views.

1. The universal catastrophic flood account holds that the flood was a worldwide event. It did indeed cover all the high mountains at that time, and it *was* catastrophic—lots of tidal waves and breaking up of the fountains of the great deep.

2. The flood was universal—it covered the whole earth—but it was a tranquil event and probably did not leave any scars or sediment on the earth.

3. The flood was just in the Mesopotamian area. Since its intent was to destroy humankind, and humankind had not spread very far, the flood only had to cover that area.

Again, as with the creation account, you need to tell your kids what your conviction is. What do *you* think about it? And, again, if you are not sure about your view, go ahead and communicate your uncertainty as well. It is okay to be uncertain about some of these things—scholars do not really know everything about them, either. And we have to be ready to realize that the kids might not like our particular interpretation, or they may have heard things in school, Sunday school, or church that may differ with our view. But it is okay to give our kids a little bit of room on these kinds of issues.

With all of these different interpretations of the Flood, what can we feel safe telling our children? What was the point of the Flood?

The purpose of the Flood of Noah was to destroy humankind as it existed at that time. Where scholars differ is in figuring out just how far people had spread. Some suggest that the human population may only have numbered a few hundred thousand, so it may have been contained in the Mesopotamian area. But if people had been around for four or five thousand years, and they had had a chance to multiply and grow, there may have been several million or tens of millions of people spread across the earth. That may be why some suggest that, in order to destroy mankind, the Flood had to be universal. But we still do not know whether it was a catastrophic or a tranquil event, and so there is some room for discussion. I think all these different theories are helpful, because they allow us to investigate God's Word to the best of our ability to determine what it really means.

One view of the Flood—the universal catastrophic flood model—has captured the attention of much of the Christian community. Several organizations propose this model. In fact, Ray, you have spent a couple of weeks in the Grand Canyon with one of these organizations investigating the flood model for the formation of the canyon. Let's address a few specifics about the catastrophic model of the Flood of Noah. Could you give just a brief outline of this model?

This catastrophic model definitely suggests a different scenario than the cute animals or the little round boat. We are talking about the breaking up of the fountains of the great deep and huge amounts of water rocking back and forth across the earth.

The young-earth creationists suggest that most of the sedimentary layers were formed during the Flood. Most of the fossils that we find in those sedimentary layers, therefore, would have been laid down as a result of the Flood of Noah. There should also be evidence around the earth of the catastrophic formation of all these sedimentary layers.

How close to the truth is the universal catastrophic flood model? Does it explain everything?

It does explain a lot of things. There is evidence for a catastrophic origin for most, if not all, sedimentary layers. Organisms seem to require a rapid burial to be formed as fossils. But there are problems with this model as well, and I think it is important that we recognize what those are.

All the different types of sediment would have to be the result of just one event, a catastrophic flood. When we look at these sedimentary layers, we have sandstone, limestone, mudstone, shale—all different types of rocks— but they all would have had to come from the same event, and that is a bit of a problem. The majority of Christian geologists believe that the strata are due to other events— like river floods or deposits from big storms and hurricanes that occurred periodically. The movement of desert sand dunes might have been the cause of sandstone layers, for example. While the catastrophic model is a captivating idea, I do not see a need to force ourselves either to accept it or reject it at this time.

A lot of work must be done concerning this model. If you have a curious, science-oriented child, why not encourage him or her to pursue a career in science and become a part of the group that investigates it?

Cavemen

Another question the kids are often curious about is, "Where do cavemen fit into the Bible?"

Most creationists believe cavemen were the early survivors of the Flood. Remember, if the purpose of the Flood was to destroy mankind, then most of these fossils would be individuals who survived it or lived soon after it. CroMagnon man and Neanderthal man, and probably even fossils described as *Homo erectus,* are all postflood humans, descendants of Noah's three sons and their wives. Their so-called primitive characteristics could be due to genetic inbreeding, faulty diet, and life in a harsh environment.

Racial Differences

Where do the different races come from? If we are all descended from one couple, Adam and Eve, why are there different colors of skin?

Races would have originated with Noah's three sons and their wives. Several sets of genes produce the wide variety of skin color present in the human population. It is not difficult at all to envision genetically similar populations becoming isolated after the Flood and being the progenitors of the different races. Much of this genetic variability may have been contained in Noah's sons' wives, arising from genetic segregation that had taken place since the creation of Adam and Eve. Adam and Eve were probably people of intermediate skin color with most, if not all, of the human variability present in their genes.

Dinosaurs

We cannot talk about explaining creation to our kids without addressing the inevitable question of the dinosaurs. Where do dinosaurs fit into the Bible?

The answer depends on your approach. There is no question that kids today, particularly boys, are enamored of dinosaurs.

From an old-earth perspective, the dinosaurs have been extinct for 70 million or so years, and there is no reason to expect them to be mentioned in the Bible at all. People and dinosaurs never existed together.

If, however, you are approaching creation from a

young-earth model, where everything was created in the fairly recent past, then dinosaurs must have existed at the same time as people because they were created on the same day, only ten to thirty thousand years ago. And that raises the question as to whether Noah took dinosaurs on the ark.

It is difficult to imagine an apatosaurus getting on the ark, and most creationists answer that by suggesting Noah probably did not take adult dinosaurs on the ark, just small juveniles. The extinction of the dinosaurs then was probably due to the Flood. Even if Noah did take some on the ark, apparently the climate and ecology of the earth had changed dramatically as the result of the Flood, and they were not able to survive following it.

But this also raises the distinct possibility that some dinosaurs may still exist in small, isolated pockets around the world. I do not want to give too much credence to this, but there are intriguing stories out there—and I just want to call them stories right now, not facts. From the Congo, different kinds of dinosaurs have been seen by villagers, and even some missionaries have reported seeing very large, reptilelike creatures in the swamps. We have cave paintings from South America of dinosaurlike creatures. We have legends all over the world about dragons—in China and the East, and in Europe dating from the Middle Ages. We seem to have it in our heads that big reptiles are out there somewhere. It would be hard to imagine an evolutionary interpretation—that they had existed in small pockets here and there during the sixty or so million years since the majority of them had become extinct. It would be easier to think they had been left over from the Flood. Also, it is possible to argue that dinosaurs are mentioned in the Bible.

✦ *Are dinosaurs referred to, then, by a different name in the Bible?*

Yes. For instance, Job 40:15–24 talks of a creature called a *behemoth.* It feeds on grass, it has strength in its loins, it has power in its belly, it has a tail like a cedar, and it ranks first among the works of God. Some think this may be a hippopotamus, but a hippopotamus does not have a tail like a cedar. And you do not think of it as ranking first among the works of God. Some suggest this could describe an apatosaur or brachiosaur. But in the next chapter, the Lord describes Leviathan to Job. Leviathan is not only a large powerful creature (most commentators have assumed it was a crocodile), but it breathed fire (Job 41:18–21). Crocodiles do not breathe fire, nor do any other creatures we know. Matthew Henry comments that this may simply be hyperbole to denote the power and terror of the wrath of God. It is possible then that these two creatures are not meant to be understood literally.

In this discussion we have tried to help you understand the biblical account of creation in the early earth so that you can explain it to your children. Although we have often presented options instead of absolutes, we can still tell our kids that God is the Creator and Sustainer of all things, and that the Flood was a real event—although some of the details may escape us at this time. This approach allows us to communicate clear biblical truth to them while at the same time encouraging their curiosity and desire to investigate. This is our Father's world, and it delights Him when His children want to discover it and search out the mysteries of the past, of history, of His story.

13

Genesis Unbound

Rich Milne

Have you ever read a book that totally changed the way you thought about something? Or heard an idea that gave you a completely new picture of something you thought you knew well? This chapter is about just such a book.

Most of us know the verses of Genesis 1 so well we could recite parts of them from memory. Some have studied them for years and read shelves of books about what the first chapters of Genesis mean. But what if someone suggested that most of what you have thought, pictured, and been told about those early chapters might not be quite right? Would you reach for the red tag of "heresy" to slap on the book? Would you be sure that the author could not possibly be right? In this discussion we are reviewing a new book called *Genesis Unbound,* and it may well cause you to reexamine what you thought Genesis 1 and 2 are about.

The author, John Sailhamer, is not a newcomer to theology. Educated at Dallas Theological Seminary and UCLA, Dr. Sailhamer taught at Trinity Evangelical Divinity School. He now teaches at Northwestern College. He has written several well-respected books on the first five books of the Bible (the Pentateuch) and is considered an excellent conservative Old Testament scholar. The commentary on Genesis in Zondervan's *Expositor's Bible Commentary* is by Dr. Sailhamer. His recent book gives a surprisingly new, and yet very old, look at the first chapters of Genesis.[1]

To lay the groundwork for any new view it is important to understand the prevailing view first. Sailhamer helpfully provides five assumptions that he says make up the core beliefs of nearly all the current views.

The first of these core assumptions is that the first verse of Genesis 1, "In the beginning God created the heavens and the earth," refers to the creation of some sort of unformed mass that God will make into a universe as the six days progress.

The second assumption that almost all commentators make about Genesis 1 is that the "light" created on day one was something unique and temporary for dividing the days until the fourth day when God created the sun, moon, and stars.

Third, it is generally assumed that the sun, moon, and stars were actually created on the fourth day.

Fourth, until recent science began to question the assumption, it had been almost universally believed that the days of Genesis 1 were normal, twenty-four-hour days. Some placed a gap between the first and second verses, in which to fit all of the geological ages, but this was not a widely held view. In our century it has been common to make the days long ages so the Bible will agree with the consensus of modern geology.

Lastly, the earth that God is making ready for man in Genesis 1 has almost always been seen as the whole planet. Accordingly, verse 1 is about the creation of the whole universe, and verse 2 begins a description of how God fashioned the earth for (a) the creatures He was about to make and (b) for the two people He would make in His own image.

But suppose there were some assumptions in this list that we did not need to make? How would that change our view of these first chapters of Genesis? We will consider this, and then look at how a Jewish reader of Moses' time might have understood Genesis 1.

The Forming of the Promised Land

We all make assumptions when we read or hear something; we cannot think without structure. But sometimes we make unnecessary assumptions that hinder our understanding. Of the five assumptions that many make about Genesis 1, could some be unnecessary baggage?

The first assumption was that "In the beginning God created the heavens and the earth" describes an initially chaotic state out of which God would create the material world. But suppose instead that this verse actually described God's creation of heaven and earth?

Sailhamer, in his book *Genesis Unbound,* carefully develops the view that in the Old Testament, the Hebrew word for "In the beginning," often describes a period of indeterminate time. Genesis 10:10 says "And the beginning of his kingdom was Babel and Erech and Accad and Calneh." Jeremiah 28:1 describes "The beginning of the reign of Zedekiah king of Judah, in the fourth year." *Genesis Unbound* suggests that we picture God creating the whole universe, "the heavens and the earth," over some unspecified time in the past.

When we begin verse 2, "And the earth was formless and void," Sailhamer says it is not talking about the whole of planet earth. What are Moses' five books about? The nation of Israel. What is the whole theme of the Pentateuch?

How God chooses a people and takes them to the Promised Land He has made for them. Why not give "earth" in verse 2 its other meaning of "land"? And why not specifically "The Land"? God, through Moses, is telling us how He prepared the Promised Land for the people He already knew He would choose. Startling?

Why, then, was the land "formless and void?" It wasn't! *Genesis Unbound* contends that this assumption crept in with the first Greek translation of the Bible, the Septuagint. It translates the Hebrew into Greek as "unseen and unformed" in order to harmonize the Bible with the view of the Greeks, who believed the world was formed out of chaos.[2] The translators wanted to seem relevant and so they mirrored that idea! According to Dr. Sailhamer, it would be better to translate the phrase as "an uninhabitable wasteland." God had not yet prepared it for people, but it was not chaos either. God was preparing to take the "wasteland" and make it the "Promised Land."

On day two, God prepares the sky for the land He will soon begin to make ready. The word often translated "firmament" Sailhamer suggests actually refers to what we would call the sky. And the waters above the firmament are the clouds that God sets in the sky. Interestingly, this is exactly what John Calvin thought. He wrote, "To my mind, this is a certain principle, that nothing is here treated of but the visible form of the world. He who would learn astronomy . . . let him go elsewhere."

On day three, God gathers together the seas and makes the dry land appear. The land is brought out of the water to make a fit place for Adam and Eve. The water settles into rivers and lakes. The Hebrew word for any body of water can be translated "sea." Here it is plural, while if it referred to the ocean it would be singular.

Then God creates "fruit trees." In Sailhamer's understanding, that is what the words describe, not all kinds of vegetation. At the end of the third day, the Promised Land has been prepared with clouds in the sky, rivers and lakes, and fruit trees for food.

The Filling of the Land

The book *Genesis Unbound* presents what seems at first a completely new understanding of Genesis 1. But by interpreting the chapter as God preparing the Promised Land, first for Adam and Eve, and eventually for His chosen nation Israel, many problems are avoided. Dr. Sailhamer takes the days to be normal twenty-four-hour days, but sees the creation of the whole universe as having taken place in the first verse, over some unstated period of time in the past. Then God focuses on preparing a place for His last creation to live.

Now, on day four, God gives a new purpose to the sun, moon, and stars that have been shining since He created them "in the beginning." On day four, God declares they are to guide the people He is about to make. They will act as measures of time; they will serve humanity. No people have been placed on earth yet, so the sun has merely been a star in the sky. Now God speaks, and the hosts of heaven take on a new function as celestial markers. On the first three days, God created the land and places for things. Now He is declaring what is to fill each part of the stage, and what their functions will be.

On day five the same word for *create* that was used in verse one occurs again: *bara*. Why does God use this word again? Dr. Sailhamer suggests that Moses is drawing our attention back to verse one to remind us that only God can create things out of nothing. But on day five, when

God populates the new land He has made, it is with animals and birds that are descendants of those He made on day one. God speaks, His creation responds, He sees it is good and blesses His creation.

Day six is the climax of the account, and the center of God's activity. Out of nothing God has created the universe in Genesis 1:1. He has prepared a special land and populated it with His creations. And then we come to people.

Here God changes His whole approach. He now announces, "Let us make man in our image." And in order for the creation to fully bear His image, He makes them male and female. Sailhamer makes an interesting point here as he discusses why the text suddenly says, "Let us." He sees a reflection of God's character in the fact that a male and female together bear God's image. Just as men and women complement one another, so too the "us" points to the relationships that exist within the Godhead.

In Dr. Sailhamer's fascinating argument in *Genesis Unbound,* when God sets out to create "in His image" for the first time, He first creates a special land for them. He then appoints the sun, moon, and stars to a new purpose, fills the land, sky, and waters with creatures, and creates a garden for Adam and Eve to live in.

Some might object that God doesn't seem to *do* very much. But, Sailhamer argues that God had already created everything out of nothing in Genesis 1:1. Now, God speaks ten times (just as He spoke the Ten Commandments) and makes a land perfect for humans to live in. He creates a garden for Adam and Eve. That garden will someday be the very land that God promises to Abraham, and eventually brings his descendents to—to Eden, the land of Israel.

Does Genesis 2 Contradict Genesis 1?

At last we come to day seven. God has created a place for each of His creations, and then God rests. He has taken a wild land, unfit for people, and has made it into a garden spot. Now, in a pattern that He sets for His creation to follow, He takes a day of rest. This becomes deeply significant later on when Moses receives the Ten Commandments.

In Exodus 20:11, God says, "For in six days the LORD made the sky, the earth, and the seas and all that is in them, and rested on the seventh day" (Sailhamer's translation). The divine pattern is to be the plan for humans as well. Even now that we are burdened with the effects of the Fall, even in our rebelliousness, God still wants His creation to rest, to take time to bless our Creator.

What, then, are we to make of Genesis 2? Many modern scholars have spoken of two creation accounts and have seen this as an inconsistency or an error in the Bible. The usual answer has been that the account in Genesis 2 narrows the focus of the account in chapter 1, that it is looking at the creation of man and woman in detail. If this is so, Dr. Sailhamer asks, then why not see Genesis 1 as describing the same place as Genesis 2, Eden? Thus he continues his argument into chapter 2.

In Genesis 2:5–6, some have seen a contradiction with the first chapter. How can there be no shrubs or plants or rain? What *Genesis Unbound* sees in these verses is a comparison being set up between before and after the Fall. There are no "shrubs of the field" or "plants of the field" because these would come as a result of Adam and Eve's disobedience. These are the "thorns and thistles" and "plants of the field" that Adam is told he must work to cultivate in Genesis 3:18–19.

When the text says "it had not rained on the earth," it

is a contrast to the time when God will "send rain on the earth" during the Flood. And there was "no man to cultivate the ground" because this too would come as a result of the Fall in Genesis 3:23. So the text is already preparing us for the results of humankind's disobedience, even as the garden is being made.

Dr. Sailhamer also finds the large amount of space devoted to locating Eden of considerable significance. While modern commentators have despaired of finding the exact place, he sees the length of the description as indicating that at least Moses expected people to know where Eden was.

The primary way that Eden is located is by the rivers that flow from it. And what are those rivers? One of them is the Pishon, a river now unknown. But the second is the Gihon, which flows around the land of Cush. Since Cush is roughly the same as Egypt, might not the river Gihon be the Nile River of Egypt? And the other two rivers are the Tigris and the Euphrates. Sailhamer thinks it is not a coincidence that two of these rivers are exactly the ones that God uses to explain to Abraham where the Promised Land will be (Gen. 15:18).

Next we will consider why Eden and Israel are so closely connected, and whether Genesis should be read as poetry or not.

Genesis Unbound and the Rest of Scripture

Genesis Unbound has many novel explanations of Genesis 1 and 2. At the same time, it helps us see how a Hebrew reader might have understood what Moses wrote, and it answers a number of puzzling questions about the text. One of these questions is, What became of Eden after God used so much care making it?

Earlier we saw how the rivers God uses to describe where Eden was are much the same as the ones He uses to tell Abraham where the Promised Land was to be. Think of the parallels. In the same way that God prepares a special place for Adam and Eve, a place they will be driven out of if they are disobedient, so too He promises first Abraham and then the whole nation of Israel a special place that they will be driven out of if they are disobedient. In fact, both are sent the same direction, to the east, when they do disobey.

And then, where will the Messiah come to? To exactly the same area where the first Adam lived! And where is the New Jerusalem of Revelation 21 located? Just where God placed the first Jerusalem—the same place that He created for Adam and Eve—Eden!

In this view, the whole Bible ties together in a way that makes complete sense and has God wasting nothing as He prepares a land for His people. The blessings and curses that form so much a part of the later books of the Pentateuch, can now be seen as foreshadowed in God's initial command to Adam and Eve.

But should we be reading Genesis so literally? After all, isn't Genesis really poetry? As an Old Testament scholar, Sailhamer makes short work of the argument. What is it that characterizes all Hebrew poetry? Parallelism and meter. Parallelism is the use of two lines to express the same idea in two ways. For example:

> The Lord is a great God
> And a great king above all gods.

These lines express the same thought in two related ways. Hebrew poetry also has a certain meter, where either the number of words or syllables will be approximately the same between two lines. Does Genesis 1 or 2 fit that pattern? Absolutely not. And in fact, Sailhamer chides evangelicals who, to try to take these chapters less literally, speak of "poetry-like" language. As he says, this seems like little more than an attempt "to dismiss the obvious intent of these narratives to tell us, in literal terms, what actually happened at creation."[3]

In conclusion, he considers the question, Is the big bang being described in Genesis 1:1? Interestingly enough, his answer is a fairly firm no. As he pointedly comments, "When understood as the 'Big Bang,' creation becomes just another example of the forces of the physical world we see around us today. . . . Our world, however, cannot be traced back to the divine act of creation. Science and history will always be separated from the divine acts of creation."[4]

You will have to read all of Dr. Sailhamer's provocative book to make up your own mind. But at least give him the chance to make his case directly from the text. *Genesis Unbound* is a book to stir your thinking and should be read slowly. But go back first and read Genesis to be reminded of God's greatness in His creation.

14

Why We Believe in Creation!

Ray Bohlin

I am often asked why the creation/evolution controversy is so important. Tempers flare, sometimes explosively, over this issue. There are enough problems with the image of evangelicals without creating unnecessary controversies. "Is it just a matter of interpreting Genesis? If so, then let the theologians debate the issues and leave me out. Just don't obscure the simple message of the gospel." "Is it just a scientific argument? If so, then why should I care about the controversy? I'm not a scientist." Well, I think much more is at stake than that. It has to do with the very nature and character of God!

We must realize that the book of Genesis is the foundation of the entire Bible. The word *genesis* means "origin" and Genesis tells the story of the beginning of the universe, solar system, earth, life, humankind, sin, Israel, nations, and salvation.[1] An understanding of Genesis is crucial to our understanding of the rest of Scripture.

For example, the first eleven chapters of Genesis are quoted or referred to more than one hundred times in the New Testament alone. And it is over these chapters that the primary battle for the historicity of Genesis rages. All of the first eleven chapters are referred to in the New

Testament. Every New Testament author refers somewhere to Genesis 1–11.[2]

Jesus Himself, on six different occasions, refers to each one of the first seven chapters of Genesis, thus affirming His belief in their historical nature. He refers to Adam and Eve to defend His position on marriage and divorce in Matthew 19:3–6. He makes His argument a historical one and affirms that Adam and Eve were real people when He says that from the beginning God created male and female.

Then Jesus affirms the historicity of Cain and Abel in Matthew 23:29–36 when He connects the blood of righteous Abel to the blood of the prophet Zechariah. The murder of Zechariah at the door of the Temple had been within the last four hundred years so was clearly part of recent history. If this was historical, then so was the murder of Abel!

Jesus confirms the historical nature of Noah and the Flood in Matthew 24:37–39. The time before Noah is related to the time that Christ returns. If the Flood is just a story to communicate a pre-New Testament vision of the gospel, then is Jesus' return just another story to communicate some other spiritual truth?

The historicity of Genesis 1–11 is tied to many aspects of Jesus' teachings. In many ways it is difficult to separate the book of Genesis (even the first eleven chapters) from the rest of Scripture, without rejecting the inspiration of Scripture and the divine nature of Jesus. It is hardly possible to assume that Jesus was knowingly deceiving the people He was talking to in order to communicate the gospel in a context they understood.

How can the first eleven chapters be separated even from the rest of Genesis? The time of Abraham has been verified by archaeology. The places, customs, and religions found in Genesis and related to Abraham are accurate. The story of Abraham begins in Genesis 12. If Genesis 1 is mythology and Genesis 12 history, where does the allegory stop and the history begin in the first eleven chapters? It is all written in the same historical narrative style.

The Nature of the Evolutionary Process

Many believers do indeed call Genesis 1–11 allegory or myth. They boldly declare that God simply used evolution as His method to create! They say the purpose of the creation account is only to promote God as a transcendent all-powerful God who is completely different from the gods of the surrounding Near East cultures of that time. This is called *theistic evolution.* Without question, God could create by any means He chose. But is the God of the Scriptures the god of evolution?

My simple answer to that question is *no*—at least not the evolution which is communicated in today's textbooks and university classrooms! The nature of the evolutionary process is contrary to the nature of God.

Behind evolution are ideas such as the selfish gene and survival of the fittest. They relate to an offshoot of evolutionary thinking, the relatively new field of sociobiology. Sociobiology is defined as the biological basis for *all* social behaviors. In other words, our behaviors are the result of natural selection as much as our physical characteristics.

For instance, if you ask a sociobiologist the question, "Why do we love our children?" he or she will answer that we love our children because it works. It is an effective means to raise productive offspring, so it was selected over time. Ultimately, then, from this perspective all behavior is selfish. Everything we do is geared toward furthering our own survival and the production and survival of our own offspring.

Our behaviors have been selected over time to aid in our survival and reproduction—and that's all.

Evolution is a wasteful, inefficient process. Carl Sagan says that the fossil record is filled with the failed experiments of evolution. Evolutionary history is littered with dead ends and false starts. Paleontologist Stephen Jay Gould characterizes the nature of the evolutionary process as one of contingency history. Organisms survive primarily by chance rather than some inherent superiority over other organisms. According to him, there is no purpose, no goal, no meaning at all.

The question has to be, "Would God use such a method?" The work we do reflects our character. A product is indicative of the mind that made it, and so is the very process that produced it. For instance, the paintings of Vincent van Gogh, their subjects, colors, and brush strokes, reveal a troubled mind. You don't have to be an art critic to see this, particularly in what he painted just before he took his own life.

God is a person and thus has character. We should see God's character in His work as well as in His method. First, let's take a brief look at the revelation of God's character.

Jesus is the perfect manifestation of God's character. Jesus said, "Anyone who has seen me has seen the Father" (John 14:9). Not only that but Jesus is the person of the Godhead that brought about the creation. Colossians 1:16 reads, "All things were created by Him and for Him." John 1:3 says, "Without Him nothing was made that has been made," and Hebrews 1:2 says, "Through Whom He made the universe." Since Jesus is then both a person and also the Creator, if He used evolution as His method of creation we should see a correlation between the character of Jesus and the process of evolution.

The Personal Character of Jesus the Creator

If Jesus used evolution as His method of creation, His character must be reconcilable with the evolutionary process. A detailed unveiling of Jesus' character is found in Matthew 5.[3] This is not an ideal we are to strive for but a description of the life of a believer who is fully yielded to Christ.

In Matthew 5:3, Jesus says, "Blessed are the poor in spirit." This phrase describes people who allow themselves to be trodden down. Jesus exemplified a security in Himself that did not become offended when He was put down. An evolutionary successful organism seeks its own interests, not the interests of others.

In verse 5, Jesus says, "Blessed are the gentle (NASB)." The mild, patient, and long-suffering are not likely to succeed in an evolutionary world. The meek are pushed aside by the self-assertive. Ultimately it is the strong, the fit, and the selfish who succeed!

In verse 7, Jesus says, "Blessed are the merciful." The struggle for existence is never motivated by mercy. Mercy could only be tolerated if shown toward a member of the same species. To be merciful outside your immediate family unit may compromise your survival or the survival of your offspring, neither of which is productive in an evolutionary world.

In verse 9, Jesus says, "Blessed are the peacemakers." Jesus also said we should love our enemies. In the case of many mammals, such as lions and gorillas, the first act of a new dominant male following his ascent to power is to kill the younger offspring sired by the previous dominant male. This has the double effect of eliminating offspring from the group that are not his and bringing their mothers into heat so he can mate with them to produce his own offspring. This is selfish natural selection at work. Where is the mercy, the gentleness, and the peacemaking in these events? The struggle for existence among living organisms today is a result of sin entering a perfect creation and is not the method of bringing that creation into existence. Romans 8:19–22 reveals that nature is longing for redemption from the Curse. Nature is in turmoil. Organisms do struggle for survival and competition is often fierce. While there are many examples of cooperation in nature, they can always be explained in terms of selfish gain in which cooperation is the easiest way to obtain the desired end. Organisms do act selfishly. But to hear nature's groaning and interpret it as the song of creation is to be ignorant of both God and nature!

Some Christians debate the effects of the Fall and how far back into earth history the effects can be realized. But the point is that something happened at the Fall. This passage makes clear that the creation does not function today as God intended it to, and it is not the creation's fault. The creation was subjected to futility because of human sin. When we take the time to investigate whether the God revealed in the Scriptures would create through the evolutionary process as it is currently understood, the answer is clear. The God of the Scriptures is not the god of evolution.

A Modern Twist on Theistic Evolution

In a modern formulation, some theistic evolutionists are declaring that not only *could* God use evolution, but He *must* use some form of evolution to create. These individuals indicate that there is a "functional integrity" to the universe that God created initially and for God to intervene in any way is to admit that He made a mistake earlier. And, of course, God does not make mistakes. Physics professor Howard van Till from Calvin College says that this is "a created world that has no functional deficiencies, no gaps in its economy of the sort that would require God to act immediately, temporarily assuming the role of creature to perform functions within the economy of the creation that other creatures have not been equipped to perform."[4]

Diogenes Allen from Princeton Theological Seminary put it this way: "According to a Christian conception of God as creator of a universe that is rational through and through, there are no missing relations between the members of nature. If, in our study of nature, we run into what seems to be an instance of a connection missing between members of nature, the Christian doctrine of creation implies that we should keep looking for one."[5]

A loose paraphrase might be: If you find evidence of a miracle, you need to keep looking for a naturalistic explanation. This view of creation seems awfully close to deism or semi-deism. Theistic evolutionists deny this, of course, by reminding us that, unlike deism, they firmly believe that God continuously upholds the universe. If He were to completely withdraw as deism holds, the universe would come apart.

But the Bible, particularly the Gospels, is full of miracles. Jesus was born as a human baby in a stable, He changed water into wine, healed blindness and leprosy, fed multitudes on scraps of food, raised people from the dead, died on a cross, and rose from the dead Himself. The response from van Till, Allen, and others is that this is salvation history which is entirely different from natural history.

According to Diogenes Allen:

In general we may say that God creates a
consistent set of law-like behaviors. As part
of that set there are the known physical
laws. These laws apply to a wide variety of
situations. But in certain unusual situations
such as creating a chosen people, revealing
divine intentions in Jesus, and revealing the
nature of the kingdom of God, higher laws
come into play that give a different outcome
than normal physical laws which concern
different situations. The normal physical
laws do not apply because we are in a domain
that extends beyond their competence.

It is true that we do not invoke God to account for
repeatable observable events such as apples falling from
trees. But what could be more unusual and beyond the
competence of physical laws than the creation of life, the
creation of coded information in DNA, the creation of a
human being. Even in this framework, it seems reasonable to assume that these events could also be a part of
salvation history. What we end up with, however, is a view
that says that the activity of the Creator cannot be detected in any of the workings of nature. Once again, the
God of the Scriptures is not the god of evolution.

The Theology of Romans 1
The world of nature that is left to us by those who
believe in theistic evolution is indistinguishable from that
of the philosophical naturalist. Pantheists could see this
perspective as compatible with their view of the natural
world as well. They see god as an impersonal force that is
present throughout nature. God is all and in all. All is
one. Matter itself, therefore, contains the inherent ability

to bring about complexity. Similarly, theistic evolution requires that matter contains within itself, by God's creative design, the full capacity to actualize all of the physical and biological complexities that exist. The distinctions of Christian theism become blurred.

Whether you accept Genesis 1 and 2 as being historical or not, the clear tenor of the narrative is of a God who interacts with His creation, not one who just lets it unwind according to some preconceived plan. How is a scientist supposed to see God in the creation if all there is from his perspective is natural mechanisms?

Finally, if God created our world through evolution, what are we to do with Romans 1:18–20. Paul says:

> For the wrath of God is revealed from heaven against all ungodliness and unrighteousness of men, who suppress the truth in unrighteousness, because that which is known about God is evident within them; for God made it evident to them. For since the creation of the world His invisible attributes, His eternal power and divine nature, have been clearly seen, being understood through what has been made, so that they are without excuse. (NASB)

God exists, and something of His power and nature are clearly understood by observing the natural world—a universe He created. If God's method of creation is indistinguishable from that described by a naturalist or a pantheist, where is this so-called evidence? Diogenes Allen says that "even though nature does not establish God's existence, nature points to the possibility of God. That is, it raises questions which science cannot answer and which philosophy has been unable to answer."[6] But Romans declares that His invisible nature, eternal power, and deity are *clearly seen through what has been made!* This is more than raising questions! If God has created through naturalistic evolution, then men and women have quite a few excuses for their behavior. If natural processes are all that are needed, who needs God?

One final interesting note. I have observed, throughout my academic career, that naturalistic evolutionists have little tolerance for theistic evolutionists. If you accept evolution, then why do you need God? Perhaps even more importantly, they don't understand why you would continue to believe in the God of the Bible if you have concluded that He used inefficient, chancy, contingent, and messy natural selection as His method for creation. Even they see the incompatibility of the two.

In summary, Genesis and creation are central to Scripture, and Jesus appears to have believed in a historic and interactive creation. If natural processes are all that is needed for life, then the claim of Romans 1, that God made His attributes clear through His creation of the world, would be false. People would have every excuse to behave as selfishly as they wished. This cannot be. Evolution is contrary to the nature and character of God.

15

Christian Views of Science and Earth History

Rich Milne and Ray Bohlin

How old is the earth? Did men live with dinosaurs? Are dinosaurs in the Bible? Where do cavemen fit in the Bible? Did the flood cover the whole earth? How many animals were on Noah's Ark? What does the word *day* in Genesis 1 mean?

These are all common and difficult questions your children may have asked. They might even be questions you have asked. What may surprise you is that evangelical Christians respond with numerous answers. In reality, these answers all depend on their answer to the first question: How old is the earth?

The diversity of opinion regarding this question inevitably leads to controversy, controversy that is often heated and remarkably lacking in grace and understanding. For those Christians who are practicing scientists, much is at stake. Not only is their view of Scripture on the firing line but the respect of the scientific community and their job security are also at risk.

We must say up front that, as important as this question is, it is secondary to defeating Darwinism as it is currently being presented to our culture. Educational leaders and evolutionary scientists are determined to present a fully naturalistic evolution as the only reasonable and scientific theory that can be discussed in the public education system. All Christians, whether old-earth or young-earth advocates, should find a common cause in their desire to dethrone philosophical naturalism as the reigning paradigm in education and science.

Returning to the age of the earth, we would like to survey three general views held among Christians today. We will discuss their positions on Genesis 1, since theological assumptions guide the process of discovering a scientific perspective. We will also discuss their scientific conclusions. Finally, we will discuss the strengths and limitations of the three views, and the opinions they have of each other.

Before we look at the positions, two things should be made clear. First, we will be painting in broad strokes. Each has many sub-categories under its umbrella. Second, we will describe the views as objectively and positively as we can without revealing our own position. We will reveal our position at the conclusion of this chapter.

Recent or Literal Creation

The first view of science and earth history we will discuss is the recent or literal view. This position is often referred to as scientific creationism, creation science, or young-earth creationism. Young-earth creationists believe that the earth and the universe are only tens of thousands of years old and that Genesis gives us a straightforward account of God's creative activity. The young-earth creationist firmly maintains that Genesis 1 is a literal, historical document that briefly outlines God's creative activity during six literal twenty-four-hour days. If one assumes that the genealogies of Genesis 5 and 11 represent a reasonable pre-Israelite history of the world, then the date of creation cannot be much beyond thirty thousand years ago.[1]

Critical to a young-earth understanding of Genesis 1 is the meaning of the Hebrew word *yom*. Translated "day" it usually refers to a literal twenty-four-hour day but also can mean an indefinite period of time, such as in the phrase "Day of the Lord." However, Henry Morris maintains that the context of Genesis makes it clear that a literal day is intended. "The writer of Genesis was trying to guard in every way possible against any of his readers deriving the notion of non-literal days from his record."[2]

A critical theological tenet of this view is that the world was free of pain, suffering, and death prior to the Fall in Genesis 3. God's prescription in Genesis 1:29 to allow only green plants and fruit for food supports this conclusion.

The universal Flood of Noah, recorded in Genesis 6 through 9, is also a crucial part of this view. The vast layers of fossil-bearing sedimentary strata found all over the earth did not have millions of years to accumulate. Therefore, the majority of these sedimentary layers are thought to have formed during Noah's Flood. Much research activity by young-earth creationists is directed along this line.[3]

Young-earth creationists also maintain the integrity of what is called the Genesis kind, defined in Genesis 1:11, 12, and 21. The dog is frequently given as an example of the Genesis kind. While this is still being researched, it is suggested that God created a population of doglike animals on the sixth day. Since then, the domestic dog, wolf, coyote, African wild dog, Australian dingo, and maybe even the fox have all descended from the original population. Young-earth creationists suggest that God created the original individual kinds with an inherent ability to diversify within that kind. But a dog cannot cross these lines to evolve into say, a cat.

This literal view of Genesis 1 has been predominant throughout church history and it proposes a testable scientific model of the Flood and the Genesis kind. Critics point out that there are immense difficulties in explaining the entire geological record in terms of the Flood.[4] Principle among these problems is that it appears there are many more animals and plants buried in the rocks than could have been alive simultaneously on the earth just prior to the Flood.

Progressive Creationism

The second position, progressive creationism or day-age creationism, holds that the earth and the universe are billions of years old. However, progressive creationists believe that God has created specifically and *ex nihilo* (out of nothing), throughout the billions of years of earth history. They do not believe that the days of Genesis refer to twenty-four-hour days, but to long, indefinite periods of time. The progressive creationist essentially believes that God has intervened throughout earth's history to bring about His creation—but not all at once over six literal twenty-four-hour days. The progressive creationist will accept the long ages of the earth and the universe while, at the same time, accepting that there is some historical significance to the creation account of Genesis.

A popular interpretation of Genesis 1 is the day-age theory. This view agrees that the events described in the first chapter of Genesis are real events, but each day is millions, perhaps billions of years in duration. The Hebrew word for day, *Yom,* can mean an indefinite period of time such as in Genesis 2:4. This verse summarizes the first thirty-four verses of the Bible by stating, "This is the account of the heavens and the earth when they were created, in the *day* that the LORD God made earth and heaven" (NASB, emphasis added). In this case, the word *day* refers to the previous seven days of the creation week. Consequently, the progressive creationists feel there is justification in rendering the days of Genesis 1 as indefinite periods of time.[5]

Because of this, progressive creationists have no problem with the standard astronomical and geological ages for the universe and the earth. A universe of 15 billion years and an earth of 4.5 billion years are acceptable. With regard to evolution, however, their position is similar to that of the young-earth creationists. Progressive creationists accept much of what would be called microevolution— adaptation within a species and even some larger changes. But macroevolutionary changes such as birds evolving from fish are not seen as a viable process.[6]

These are the basic beliefs of most progressive creationists. What do they think is the predominant reason for holding to this perspective? Most will tell you that the evidence for an old universe and earth is so strong that they have needed to find a way to fit Genesis 1 into this framework. So agreement with standard geology and astronomy is critical to them. Progressive creationists also find the biblical evidence for God's creative activity unassailable. The lack of macroevolutionary evidence dovetails well with that.

The most difficult problem for them is the requirement that pain, suffering, and death must have been a necessary part of God's creation prior to Adam's sin. The atheistic evolutionist from Harvard, Stephen Jay Gould, commented on this problem when he said, "The price of perfect design is messy relentless slaughter."[7] There are also major differences between the order of events in earth history and the order given in Genesis. For instance, if the days of Genesis are millions of years long, then although flowers were created on day three, it would be millions of years before pollinators, such as bees, were created—on days five and six.

Theistic Evolution

A view traditionally known as theistic evolution comprises the third position. Theistic evolutionists essentially believe that the earth and the universe are not only billions of years old but that there was little, if any, intervention by God during this time. The universe and life have evolved by God-ordained processes in nature. Most theistic evolutionists, or evolutionary creationists, as many prefer to be called, believe that the first chapter of Genesis is meant to be a description of God as the perfect Creator. Most see little, if any, historical significance to the opening chapters of Genesis. They suggest that the narrative was designed to show the Israelites that there is one God and that He created everything, including those things which the surrounding nations worshipped as gods. In essence, Genesis 1 is religious and theological, not historical and scientific.[8]

Another view of creation, which has become popular with progressive creationists as well as theistic evolutionists, is the structural framework hypothesis.[9] In the ancient Near East it was believed that a perfect work was completed in six days with a seventh for rest, the six days being divided into three groups of two days each. The seven days of biblical creation fit into this framework. At the beginning the earth was formless and void, as stated in Genesis 1:2. The first three days of creation removed the formlessness of the earth, and the last three days filled the void of the earth. On days one through three God created light, sea and sky, and the land. On days four through six, God filled the heavens, sky, sea, and land. Thus, in Genesis 1 we have six days of work with a seventh day of rest, though unlike the Near Eastern framework the six days are divided into two groups of three days. Still, perhaps the narrative framework of the Genesis story itself was emphasizing that God is the Creator and His work is perfect. Unfortunately, what we don't possess is a commentary from the second millennium B.C. to tell us how the early Israelites understood the passage.

Essentially, theistic evolutionists accept nearly all the scientific data of evolution, including the age of the cosmos and the evolutionary relatedness of all living creatures. God either guided evolution or created the evolutionary process so that it could proceed without further need for interference.

Theistic evolutionists maintain that the evidence for evolution is so strong that they have simply reconciled their faith with reality. Since reading Genesis historically does not agree with what they perceive to be the truth about earth history, then Genesis, if it is to be considered God's Word, must mean something else. They do believe that God is continually upholding the universe, so He is involved in His creation.

Theistic evolution has the same problem with pain, suffering, and death before the Fall that progressive creation does.[10] In addition, the origin of life, of major groups of organisms, and of human beings are all severe problems for the theistic evolutionist, as they are for the secular evolutionist.[11] Some theistic evolutionists also quarrel with a literal Adam and Eve. If humans evolved from apelike ancestors, then who were Adam and Eve? If Adam and Eve were not literal people, then is the Fall real? And how is redemption necessary if they are imaginary?

Call for Caution and Discussion

We have discussed the biblical and scientific foundations for three Christian views of science and earth history. In doing so, we have tried to convey both their strengths and their limitations. Our intention has been to present them as objectively as possible so you can make an informed decision. We have purposefully kept our own views out of this discussion. Now we would like to explain our position.

We have studied this issue for over twenty years and have read scholarly books, both biblical and scientific, from every side of the question. For some ten years now, we have been confirmed fence-sitters. Yes, we are sorry to disappoint those of you who were waiting for us to tell you which view makes more sense—but we are decidedly undecided. This is by no means a political decision. We are not trying to please all sides, because if that were the case, we know we would please no one. The fact is, we are still searching.

From a biblical perspective the young-earth approach, with six consecutive twenty-four-hour days of creation and a catastrophic universal flood, makes the most sense. However, we have found the scientific evidence that the universe and the earth are of great age is nearly overwhelming. We just do not know how to resolve the conflict yet. Earlier, we said that the age of the earth, the time frame during which God accomplished His creation, was *not* the primary question in the origins debate. In reality the foremost question is that of chance versus design.

Such indecision is not necessarily a bad thing. Davis Young in his book, *Christianity and the Age of the Earth*, gives a wise caution. Young explains that both science and theology have mysteries that remain unsolvable. And if each has its own mystery, how can we expect them to mesh perfectly?[12] For instance, as Christians we believe in the Trinity. God is one, but also three persons. And science maintains that light is both a wave and a particle at the same time. Neither of these things can be explained, yet we hold them to be true. The great twentieth-century evangelist Francis Schaeffer said: "We must take ample time, and sometimes this will mean a long time, to consider whether the apparent clash between science and revelation means that the theory set forth by science is wrong or whether we must reconsider what we thought the Bible says."[13]

In the sixteenth century, Michelangelo sculpted Moses (1513–1515) coming down from Mount Sinai with two prominent bumps on his head. The word that describes Moses' face as he came off the mountain we now know means "shining light." Moses' face was brilliant from having been in God's presence. But in the sixteenth century this meaning was unknown. The only Hebrew word close in spelling was the root word for goat horns. So Michelangelo sculpted Moses with two horns on his head. This didn't make much sense, but that's what the scholars of the day thought the Bible literally said. Now we know better, and we have changed our interpretation of this passage based on more accurate information.

More accurate information is needed, both from the Bible and from science, to answer the question of the age of the earth. Ultimately, we believe there is a resolution to this dilemma. All truth is God's truth. Some suggest that perhaps God has created a universe with apparent age. That is certainly possible, but particular implications of this make us very uncomfortable. It is true that any form of creation out of nothing implies some form of apparent age. God created Adam as an adult who appeared to have been alive for several decades, though only a few seconds into his existence.

Scientists have observed supernova from galaxies that are hundreds of thousands of light years away. We know that many of these galaxies must be this distant because if they were all within a few thousand light years, the night-time sky would be brilliant indeed. The explanation for this is usually that God created the light in transit so we could see it today. However, we have observed events in these distant galaxies—events such as supernova. These star explosions come to us with all the accompanying radiation and with every appearance of a real explosion. But if the galaxy is millions of light years away and the light had to be created in transit for us to see it, this means that the explosion never happened in an apparent age universe. Therefore, we are viewing an event that never occurred. This would be like God giving us a videotape of Adam's birth. Would supernovas that never happened make God deceptive?

We believe we must approach this question with humility. We must have tolerance for those with different convictions. The truth will eventually be known. In the meantime, let us search for it together without snipping at each other's heels.

Endnotes

Chapter 1

1. Pierre P. Grassé, *Evolution of Living Organisms* (New York: Academic Press, 1977), 87.
2. Charles B. Thaxton, Walter L. Bradley, and Roger L. Olsen, *The Mystery of Life's Origin* (Dallas: Lewis and Stanley, 1984), 66.
3. Walter L. Bradley and Charles B. Thaxton, "Information and the Origin of Life," in *The Creation Hypothesis: Scientific Evidence of an Intelligent Designer,* ed. J. P. Moreland (Downers Grove, Ill.: InterVarsity, 1994), 173–210.
4. Klaus Dose, "The Origin of Life: More Questions Than Answers," *Interdisciplinary Science Review* 13 (1988): 348–56.
5. Bradley and Thaxton, "Information and the Origin of Life," 209.
6. Richard Dawkins, *Climbing Mount Improbable* (New York: W. W. Norton, 1996), 162–63.
7. Wallace Arthur, *Theories of Life* (London: Pelican, 1987), 180.
8. Wallace Arthur, *The Origin of Animal Body Plans: A Study in Evolutionary Developmental Biology* (Cambridge, U.K.: Cambridge Univ. Press, 1997), 22.
9. Keith Stewart Thomson, "Macroevolution: The Morphological Problem," *American Zoologist* 32 (1992): 106–12.
10. Michael J. Behe, *Darwin's Black Box: The Biochemical Challenge to Evolution* (New York: Free Press, 1996).
11. Richard Dawkins, *The Blind Watchmaker* (New York: W. W. Norton, 1986), 1.
12. Ibid., 21.
13. Ibid., 89–90.
14. Phillip E. Johnson, *Reason in the Balance: The Case Against Naturalism in Science, Law, and Education* (Downers Grove, Ill.: InterVarsity, 1995), 80–82.
15. Stephen J. Gould, "The Episodic Nature of Evolutionary Change," in *The Panda's Thumb* (New York: W. W. Norton, 1980), 181.
16. Stephen J. Gould and Niles Eldredge, "Punctuated Equilibria: The Tempo and Mode of Evolution Reconsidered," *Paleobiology* 3 (1977): 116.
17. Barbara J. Stahl, *Vertebrate History: Problems in Evolution* (New York: Dover, 1985), 121–48.

Chapter 2

1. George Gallup Poll, quoted in "Darwinism's Rules of Reasoning," in *Darwinism: Science or Philosophy,* by Phillip Johnson (Richardson, Tex.: Foundation for Thought and Ethics, 1994), 10.
2. William Howells, *Getting Here: The Story of Human Evolution* (Washington, D.C.: The Compass Press, 1993), 79.
3. Roger Lewin, *Principles of Human Evolution* (Malden, Mass.: Blackwell Science, 1998), 249.
4. Marvin L. Lubenow, *Bones of Contention: A Creationist Assessment of the Human Fossils* (Grand Rapids: Baker, 1992), 21.
5. Richard Leakey and Roger Lewin, *Origins Reconsidered: In Search of What Makes Us Human* (New York: Doubleday, 1992), 83–84.
6. Ibid., 137–72.
7. Lubenow, *Bones of Contention,* 17.
8. Ibid., 36–39.
9. William Howells, quoted in Lubenow, *Bones of Contention,* 56–57.
10. Donald Johanson and Blake Edgar, *From Lucy to Language* (New York: Simon and Schuster, 1996), 40.
11. Leakey and Lewin, *Origins Reconsidered,* 103.
12. Howells, *Getting Here,* 79.
13. Johanson and Edgar, *From Lucy to Language,* 132.
14. Lubenow, *Bones of Contention,* 247–66.
15. Ibid., 266.
16. Johanson and Edgar, *From Lucy to Language,* 247; Lubenow, *Bones of Contention,* 153–56.
17. Arthur Custance, *Genesis and Early Man* (Grand Rapids: Zondervan, 1975), 202–4.
18. Lubenow, *Bones of Contention,* 144–56.

Chapter 3

1. Lane P. Lester and Raymond G. Bohlin, *The Natural Limits to Biological Change* (Richardson, Tex.: Probe Books, 1984).
2. Pierre P. Grassé, *Evolution of Living Organisms* (New York: Academic Press, 1977), 87.
3. Jerry A. Coyne, "Not Black and White," *Nature* 396 (5 November 1998): 35–36.
4. Barbara J. Stahl, *Vertebrate History: Problems in Evolution* (New York: Dover, 1985), 121–48.
5. Stephen J. Gould and Niles Eldredge, "Punctuated Equilibrium Comes of Age," *Nature* 366 (1993): 266.
6. Michael J. Behe, *Darwin's Black Box* (New York: Free Press, 1996).
7. Walter L. Bradley and Charles B. Thaxton, "Information and the Origin of Life," in *The Creation Hypothesis: Scientific Evidence of an Intelligent Designer,* ed. J. P. Moreland (Downers Grove, Ill.: InterVarsity, 1994), 173–210.
8. William A. Dembski, ed., *Mere Creation: Science, Faith, and Intelligent Design* (Downers Grove, Ill.: InterVarsity, 1998); and idem, *The Design Inference: Eliminating Chance Through Small Probabilities* (Cambridge, U.K.: Cambridge Univ. Press, 1998).

9. Jonathan Wells, "Unseating Naturalism," in *Mere Creation: Science, Faith, and Intelligent Design,* 62–66.
10. Michael Denton, *Evolution: A Theory in Crisis* (Bethesda, Md.: Adler and Adler, 1985), 113–15.
11. John W. Oller Jr. and John L. Omdahl, "Origin of the Human Language Capacity: In Whose Image?" in *The Creation Hypothesis: Scientific Evidence of an Intelligent Designer,* 252.
12. Ibid., 254.

Chapter 4

1. J. Madeleine Nash, "When Life Exploded," *Time* 146, no. 23 (4 December 1995): 66–74.
2. Ibid., 67.
3. Ibid., 70.
4. Ibid.
5. Richard Lewontin, "Adaptation," *Scientific American* 239 (September 1978): 213.
6. D. G. Shu, et al., "Lower Cambrian Vertebrates from South China," *Nature* 402 (4 November 1999): 42–46.
7. Jonathan Wells, "Recent Insights from Developmental Biology," in *Mere Creation: Science, Faith and Intelligent Design,* ed. William A. Dembski (Downers Grove, Ill.: InterVarsity, 1998), 53–58.
8. Nash, "When Life Exploded," 73.
9. Ibid., 74.
10. Lane P. Lester and Raymond G. Bohlin, *The Natural Limits to Biological Change* (Richardson, Tex.: Probe Books, 1984).
11. Martin Wolf, "Letters," *Time* 146, no. 26 (25 December 1995– 1 January 1996): 10.
12. Andrew M. Koenigsberg, "Letters," in Ibid.
13. Doug West, "Letters," in Ibid.
14. Dembie Copenhaver, "Letters," in Ibid.
15. Stephen J. Gould, *Wonderful Life: The Burgess Shale and the Nature of History* (New York: W. W. Norton, 1989), 217.

Chapter 5

1. A full review of this book can be found in an article of the same title and author in the journal, *Creation Ex Nihilo Technical Journal* 10, no. 3 (1996): 322–27.
2. Richard Dawkins, *A River Out of Eden: A Darwinian View of Life* (New York: Basic Books, 1995), 12.
3. Ibid., 43.
4. Ibid., 44.
5. Michael J. Behe, "Histone Deletion Mutants Challenge the Molecular Clock Hypothesis," *Trends in Biochemical Science* 15 (1990): 374–76.
6. Dawkins, *River Out of Eden,* 70.
7. Ibid., 84.
8. Ibid., 91.

9. Ibid., 96.
10. Ibid., 131.
11. Ibid., 138.
12. Charles B. Thaxton, Walter L. Bradley, and Roger L. Olsen, *The Mystery of Life's Origin: Reassessing Current Theories* (Dallas: Lewis and Stanley, 1984); and Walter L. Bradley and Charles B. Thaxton, "Information and the Origin of Life," in *The Creation Hypothesis: Scientific Evidence of an Intelligent Designer,* ed. J. P. Moreland (Downers Grove, Ill.: InterVarsity, 1994), 173–210.

Chapter 6

1. Carl Sagan, *Contact* (New York: Pocket Books [Simon and Schuster], 1986).
2. Carl Sagan, *The Demon-Haunted World* (New York: Ballantine Books, 1996), 459.
3. Sagan, *Contact,* 20.
4. Carl Sagan, *Cosmos,* "Episode 1: The Shores of the Cosmic Ocean" Turner Home Entertainment, 1989, videocassette.
5. Ibid.
6. Carl Sagan, *Cosmos* (New York: Random House, 1980), 4.
7. Carl Sagan, *Billions and Billions* (New York: Random House, 1997), 225.
8. Ibid., 228.

Chapter 7

1. David S. McKay, Everett K. Gibson, Kathis L. Thomas-Keprta, Hojatollah Vali, Christopher S. Romanek, Simon J. Clement, Xavier D. F. Chillier, Claude R. Maechling, and Richard N. Zare, "Search for Past Life on Mars: Possible Relic Biogenic Activity in Martian Meteorite ALH84001," *Science* 273 (16 August 1996): 924–30.
2. Ralph P. Harvery and Harry Y. McSween, "A Possible High-Temperature Origin for the Carbonates in the Martian Meteorite ALH84001," *Nature* 382 (4 July 1996): 49–51.
3. William Schopf, quoted in "Ancient Life on Mars?" by Richard A. Kerr, *Science* 273 (16 August 1996): 864.
4. McKay et al., "Search for Past Life on Mars," 929.
5. Hugh Ross, *Creator and the Cosmos* (Colorado Springs: NavPress, 1995), 155.
6. Ibid., 111–45.
7. Charles B. Thaxton, Walter L. Bradley, and Roger L. Olsen, *The Mystery of Life's Origin: Reassessing Current Theories* (Dallas: Lewis and Stanley, 1984).
8. Walter L. Bradley and Charles B. Thaxton, "Information and the Origin of Life," in *The Creation Hypothesis: Scientific Evidence of an Intelligent Designer,* ed. J. P. Moreland (Downers Grove, Ill.: InterVarsity, 1994), 173–210.
9. Carl Sagan, *Cosmos* (New York: Random House, 1980), 40.
10. Christian de Duve, *Vital Dust: Life as a Cosmic Imperative* (New York: Basic Books, 1995), 9.

Chapter 8

1. Phillip E. Johnson, *Defeating Darwinism by Opening Minds* (Downers Grove, Ill: InterVarsity, 1997).
2. Phillip E. Johnson, *Darwin on Trial,* 2d ed. (Downers Grove, Ill: InterVarsity, 1993).
3. Phillip E. Johnson, *Reason in the Balance* (Downers Grove, Ill: InterVarsity, 1995).
4. Michael Denton, *Evolution: A Theory in Crisis* (Bethesda, Md.: Adler and Adler, 1985).
5. Johnson, *Defeating Darwinism,* 38.
6. Ibid., 54.
7. Ibid., 35.
8. Ibid., 33.
9. Ibid., 45.
10. Ibid., 10.
11. Quoted in Ibid., 77.
12. Ibid.
13. Quoted in Ibid., 81.
14. Ibid., 114.
15. Ibid., 113.
16. Ibid., chap. 8.
17. Ibid., 118.

Chapter 9

1. Charles Darwin, *On the Origin of Species,* 6th ed. (1872; reprint, New York: New York Univ. Press, 1988), 154.
2. Tom Woodward, The 1997 Book Awards, *Christianity Today* 41, no. 5 (28 April 1997): 12–13.
3. Michael J. Behe, *Darwin's Black Box* (New York: Free Press, 1996), 223.
4. Ibid., 179.
5. Jerry Coyne, "God in the Details," *Nature* 383 (19 September 1996): 227–28.

Chapter 10

1. Raymond G. Bohlin, "Sociobiology: Cloned from the Gene Cult," *Christianity Today,* 23 January 1981, 16–19.
2. Edward O. Wilson, *Consilience: The Unity of Knowledge* (New York: Random House, 1998), 246–47.
3. Ibid., 4–6; and Edward O. Wilson, *The Naturalist* (Washington, D.C.: Island Press), 33–46. On pages 45–46 Wilson recalls an event that indicates his continuing struggle with his evangelical past. After hearing a choir of black Harvard students sing a medley of old-time gospel hymns in 1984, he finds himself weeping. "My people, I thought. My people. And what else lay hidden deep within my soul?"
4. Robert Wallace, *The Genesis Factor* (New York: Morrow and Co., 1979).
5. E. O. Wilson, *Sociobiology: The New Synthesis* (Cambridge, Mass.: Harvard Univ. Press, 1975), 3.
6. E. O. Wilson, *On Human Nature* (Cambridge, Mass.: Harvard Univ. Press, 1978), 2–3.

7. Ibid., 217–18. Emphasis mine.
8. William Irons, "How Did Morality Evolve?" *Zygon* 26 (1991): 49–89.
9. Bohlin, "Sociobiology," 19.

Chapter 11

1. Andrew Dickson White, *A History of the Warfare of Science with Theology in Christendom,* 2 vols. (1896; reprint, New York: Dover Publications, 1960).
2. Nancy R. Pearcey and Charles B. Thaxton, *The Soul of Science: Christian Faith and Natural Philosophy* (Wheaton, Ill.: Crossway, 1994), 17–42.
3. Richard Dawkins, *The Blind Watchmaker: Why the Evidence of Evolution Reveals a Universe Without Design* (New York: W. W. Norton, 1986), 6.
4. Carl Sagan, *Cosmos* (New York: Random House, 1980), 4.
5. Stephen Jay Gould, "Nonoverlapping Magisteria," *Natural History* 106, no. 2 (March 1997): 16–22, 60–62.
6. Ibid., 19.
7. John Paul II, "Truth Cannot Contradict Truth," http://www.sni.netfadventdocs/ip02tc.htm (1996): point 4, par. 1.
8. Gould, "Nonoverlapping Magisteria," 61.
9. John Paul II, "Truth Cannot Contradict Truth," point 4, pars. 2–3.
10. Ibid., point 4, par. 4.
11. Ibid., point 5, par. 1.
12. Ibid.
13. Gould, "Nonoverlapping Magisteria," 16.
14. John Paul II, "Truth Cannot Contradict Truth," point 2, par. 1.
15. Gould, "Nonoverlapping Magisteria," 62.

Chapter 12

1. David Raup, "Conflicts Between Darwin and Paleontology," *Field Museum of Natural History Bulletin* 30, no. 1 (1979): 25.
2. A. H. Brush, "On the origin of feathers," *Journal of Evolutionary Biology* 9 (1996): 132.
3. Elizabeth Pennisi, "Haeckel's Embryos: Fraud Rediscovered," *Science* 277 (5 September 1997): 1435.
4. Kenneth Miller and Joseph Levine, *Biology* (Englewood Cliffs, N.J.: PrenticeHall, 1991), 343–44.
5. Klaus Dose, "The Origin of Life: More Questions Than Answers," *Interdisciplinary Science Review* 13 (1988): 348–56.
6. Stephen J. Gould, *The Panda's Thumb* (New York: Norton, 1980), 181.
7. Jerry Coyne, "Not Black and White," *Nature* 396 (5 November 1998): 35–36.
8. Peter R. Grant and B. Rosemary Grant, "Hybridization of Bird Species," *Science* 256 (10 April 1992): 193–97.
9. Miller and Levine, *Biology,* 335.
10. Marvin Lubenow, *Bones of Contention* (Grand Rapids: Baker, 1992).

Chapter 13

1. John Sailhamer, *Genesis Unbound* (Sisters, Ore: Multnomah, 1996).
2. Ibid., ch. 11 n4, Sailhamer here quotes John Calvin, *Commentaries*

on the First Book of Moses Called Genesis, trans. J. King (Grand Rapids: Baker, 1979), 86.
3. Ibid., 234.
4. Ibid., 244–45.

Chapter 14

1. Henry Morris, *The Genesis Record* (Grand Rapids: Baker, 1976), 18–21.
2. Ibid., 21.
3. A. E. Wilder-Smith, *Man's Origin, Man's Destiny* (Wheaton, Ill.: Harold Shaw, 1968), 167–73.
4. Howard van Till, *Christian Scholars Review* 22 (September 1991): 38.
5. Diogenes Allen, *Christian Belief in a Postmodern World* (Louisville: Westminster/John Knox, 1989), 53.
6. Ibid., 180.

Chapter 15

1. Henry Morris, *The Genesis Record* (Grand Rapids: Baker, 1976), 37–81.
2. Ibid., 55–57.
3. Steven A. Austin, ed., *Grand Canyon: Monument to Catastrophe* (Santee, Calif.: Institute for Creation Research, 1994), 284.
4. Daniel E. Wonderly, *Neglect of Geologic Data: Sedimentary Strata Compared with Young-Earth Creationist Writings* (Hatfield, Pa.: Interdisciplinary Biblical Research Institute, 1987), 130; and Howard J. van Till, Robert Snow, John Stek, and Davis A. Young, *Portraits of Creation: Biblical and Scientific Perspectives on the World's Formation* (Grand Rapids: Eerdmans, 1990), 26–125.
5. Hugh Ross, *Creation and Time* (Colorado Springs: NavPress, 1994), 45–72.
6. Ibid., 73–80.
7. Stephen Jay Gould, "Darwin and Paley Meet the Invisible Hand," *Natural History,* November 1990, 8; and Mark Van Bebber and Paul S. Taylor, *Creation and Time: A Report on the Progressive Creationist Book by Hugh Ross* (Mesa, Ariz.: Eden Comm., 1994), 128.
8. Van Till et al., *Portraits of Creation,* 232–42.
9. Umberto Cassuto, *A Commentary on the Book of Genesis: Part 1: From Adam to Noah,* trans. Israel Abrahams (Jerusalem: Magnum Press, 1978), 12–17; and Henri Blocher, *In the Beginning: The Opening Chapters of Genesis,* trans. David G. Preston (Downers Grove, Ill.: InterVarsity, 1984), 49–59.
10. Ken Ham, *Evolution: The Lie* (El Cajon, Calif.: Creation-Life, 1987).
11. Phillip E. Johnson, *Darwin on Trial,* 2d ed. (Downers Grove, Ill.: InterVarsity, 1993), 15–112, 166–70.
12. Davis A. Young, *Christianity and the Age of the Earth* (Grand Rapids: Zondervan, 1982), 158.
13. Francis Schaeffer, *No Final Conflict* (Downers Grove, Ill.: InterVarsity, 1975), 24.